The Art of the Laugh

The ART of the LAUGH

*A handbook
for sketch writers,
actors, and directors*

based on the traditions of the Brave New Workshop Theatre

Aerialist
Press

The Art of the Laugh © copyright 2005 John Sweeney.
All rights reserved.

ISBN 0-9762184-1-0

Library of Congress Catalog Number: 2005926751

Published in the United States of America
Printed in Canada

First Printing: September 2005

09   08   07   06   05   5   4   3   2   1

Dustjacket design by Kyle G. Hunter
Book design by Ann Sudmeier
Edited by Jeni Henrickson
Composition by Stanton Publication Services, Inc.

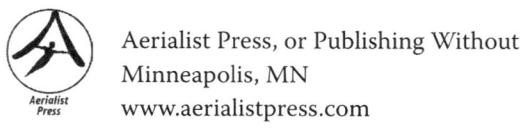

Aerialist Press, or Publishing Without a Net
Minneapolis, MN
www.aerialistpress.com

*The book is dedicated to Dudley Riggs
and anyone who has ever worked
at the Brave New Workshop,
and to Jenni Lilledahl, my wife
and lifelong improv teacher*

Acknowledgments

This book would not have been possible were it not for the wonderful people at the Brave New Workshop. I am grateful to all of them. To Troy Alexander, for suggesting that I write this book, but, especially, to Dawn Hopkins.

Contents

- xi Foreword *by Pat Proft*
- xv Preface

Part 1: An Introduction
- 3 What is the Brave New Workshop?
- 5 What is Improvisation?

Part 2: The 8 Secrets of BNW Creativity
- 12 Secret 1   Accept All Ideas
- 18 Secret 2   Defer Judgment
- 25 Secret 3   Share Focus & Accept All Styles
- 31 Secret 4   Declarations
- 37 Secret 5   Create a Statusless Environment
- 44 Secret 6   Create a Reward System That Recognizes Innovation & Creative Risk-Taking
- 49 Secret 7   Yes, First!
- 54 Secret 8   Perceive Change as Fuel

Part 3: Especially for the Sketch Writer
- 59 Getting Started
- 61 The Sketch-Writing Process

Part 4: Practical Applications
- 69 Idea Generation and the Creative Funnel Process
- 81 The Miracle of Imperfection
- 81 The BNW Rehearsal Process
- 87 Where Do I Go from Here?
- 89 Insights from Everyday Actors, Writers, and Teachers

- 99   Appendix 1:   Form to organize the key elements of your sketch
- 103 Appendix 2:   Sample sketch, from first draft through final sketch
- 123 Appendix 3:   Other sample sketches
- 139 Appendix 4:   The Brave New Workshop, Yesterday & Today

- 145 Index
- 149 CD Content

Foreword

by Pat Proft

Welcome to a book. Not just a book . . . well, yeah, it is just a book. But inside, John Sweeney has laid before your very eyes . . . or eye, I mean, accidents do happen . . . a sorta, kinda, how-to, or how they do it at the Brave New Workshop when it comes to putting together comedy material. I'd say a big part of the success of writing great comedy is sex the day before. But when I come to my senses, I agree with John Sweeney, it's improvisation.

But enough about John Sweeney. Let's talk about me. Since 1965 I've been paid to perform or write comedy. Not bad. It's allowed me to see many exotic and mystical cities like Edmonton, Calgary, and Moose Jaw. And my name is known throughout the movie-going world. Once, while being interviewed on a French Big Time Radio Show (All Surrender Radio 1940), I was told I look like Woody Woodpecker. Gee, aren't the French fun? It just don't get no better than that.

A few key things made my life easier, two great parents and one Dudley Riggs and his Brave New Workshop. I jumped into the cast of the BNW in June 1965. We had scripts, great satirical sketches written by Irv Letofsky. Over the days of rehearsals and previews in front of audiences, I got to throw a few of my ideas into the sketches. Ad lib here. Toss a dumb something there. Cast members would give me an idea and I'd toss it in the mix. And a funny piece became funnier through improvisation. Aha, perhaps this is the way to approach writing sketches.

In my years at the BNW, from 1965 to 1969, we were at the theatre about a million hours a week. And we loved it. As soon as we got a show up and running, we started putting together the next revue. If we hadn't had Irv writing, Jim Wallace directing, and the cast improvising material, it would have been an impossible task to come up with a new show every ten weeks. And that's a show with ninety minutes of solid comedy. Belly laughs I can still remember. In fact, for big laugh memories, the opening night of *The Naked Gun* and the BNW's "All Dirty Revue" are in a dead heat in my mind. So there.

With John Sweeney's years at the BNW, he has perfected a great working formula that has given birth to an environment that makes comedy click. In the past five years, I've seen moments at the BNW I wish I had come up with. And now I have! The BNW and I are in the process of grabbing some of those moments and building a movie around them. So stay tuned.

I wanted to switch back to me again, but I think I blew my wad. Back to John Sweeney. No wait . . . me! The movies I've written with the team of ZAZ (Zucker/Abrahams/Zucker)—that would be the "Naked Guns"—were done with improvisation. We'd throw ideas at each other and riff on them. When they would make us laugh, they would make the movie. In fact, every film I've cowritten, from *Police Academy* and *Bachelor Party* with Neal Israel, to *Scary Movie 3* with Craig Mazin and director David Zucker, were all done by sitting in a room working premises, tossing ideas, forming jokes, and coming up with a script—the same process we were doing at the BNW for years.

By the way, no idea is a bad idea. Every idea is recorded. A lot of times the discards are brought back to form the backbone of a joke or a scene. I've learned to never say never about any idea. So there (again). By the way, John Sweeney agrees. Great, now we're back to John. And well we should be.

You can't teach being funny, but John Sweeney's *The Art of the Laugh* is a good guide to putting a good piece of material together. Honest. For real. No kiddin'. You betcha.

As Always I Am Always,
Pat Proft

Pat's Screenplays:
- *Police Academy*
- *Bachelor Party*
- *Real Genius*
- *Moving Violations*
- *Lucky Stiff*
- *The Naked Gun*
- *The Naked Gun 2½: The Smell of Fear*
- *Hot Shots!*
- *Brain Donors*
- *Hot Shots! Part Deux*
- *Naked Gun 33⅓: The Final Insult*
- *High School High*
- *Mr. Magoo*
- *Wrongfully Accused*
- *Scary Movie 3*

Some TV Stuff:
- *Police Squad!*
- Steve Martin, Mary Tyler Moore, Bob Hope, Dick Van Dyke, Smothers Brothers, Carol Burnett, Redd Foxx

Preface

In early 1991, I began taking classes in the art of improvisational theatre, mostly as a stress reliever I guess. I was probably working a little too hard and needed something to distract me from the daily grind of corporate real estate. Life wasn't bad though. I had a great house, a high-paying job, and an exceptional social life. I thought that taking a class in improvisation might also be a way to fulfill my need to be "the funny guy."

I remember everything about that first class—every exercise we did and, most importantly, every emotion I felt as I became more excited, more curious, and more intrigued with this quirky little art form. In the next two years, I became consumed with improvisation. I couldn't get enough. It seemed more than just a vehicle to perform; it stirred me, it was undeniable.

In October 1993, it seemed as though I was fully addicted to improvisation as I made the decision to leave the fortieth floor of the IDS Tower in Minneapolis, Minnesota, and my job as a commercial real estate consultant, to become a full-time resident member of the Dudley Riggs Brave New Workshop Comedy Theatre. My starting salary was $200 per week, before taxes. I sold my home, turned in my company car, and started driving a 1989 Bonneville that my brother gave me. I had no idea where this improvisational path would lead, but I knew that if I didn't follow it, it would be something I'd regret for the rest of my life. So there I was—twenty-eight, single, and a full-time comedic actor. Where would this lead me?

Eleven years later, my wife Jenni Lilledahl and I own that very same theatre. We have a wonderful marriage, a beautiful new son, and a life we wouldn't change for anything. If I had to attribute this phenomenal journey to one thing, it would be improvisation. Since that first class, I have slowly incorporated the values and principles of improvisation into my stage work, my writing, my relationships, and how I run my business.

In March 1997, when we purchased the Brave New Workshop Theatre from its founder, Dudley Riggs, it had gross revenues of a little over $200,000 per year. Eight years later, we will exceed $2 million per year. We have grown this wonderful company from five employees to more than fifty on our weekly payroll list. The educational arm of the company, the Brave New Institute, has expanded from twelve to more than 275 students. Our corporate services division has grown from almost nonexistence to become a national leader in corporate entertainment, training, and keynote speaking.

I wish I could say that this level of growth and success is a clear representation of my competence, vision, and managerial skills. The truth is, in all three areas, I am average at best. Improvisation is the reason we have achieved such success. If I have done anything to play a role in the last ten years of my life, it would be that I have been able to bridge my understanding of improvisational theatre into both the personal and business sides of my life. By simply following the secrets you are about to read, I have been able to surround myself with incredibly competent and loyal employees and to produce entertainment and training programs that generally surpass our audiences' and clients' expectations.

The core of the BNW has always been the live sketch comedy we have performed for our audiences. Since 1958 we have been able to create thought-provoking social and political satire on our stages. The process of creating our scripts is as unique as our theatre or the material that we produce. By refining and documenting this process we were able to maintain our high standard of artistic integrity while increasing the efficiency and speed with which we produce our sketches.

My hope is that you will be able to use these same secrets to improve your innovation and the quality of your creative work and your life. Hang on and enjoy the ride.

The Art of the Laugh

Part 1
An Introduction

What is the Brave New Workshop?

Since 1958, the Brave New Workshop (BNW) has created smart, edgy, and innovative comedy on a yearly, monthly, weekly, daily, and sometimes hourly basis. If you were to stand in the lobby of our small, storefront theatre after one of our shows, you'd hear the following comments: "How did they think of that?" "This show was better than the last show!" "How do they come up with that stuff?" "That was the funniest thing I have ever seen!" We've been consistently hearing these comments from more than 3 million customers for over forty-seven years.

Brave New Workshop staff, instructors, writers, and performers have developed the secrets of a unique brand of improvisation—and the principles and philosophies that go with it—for generations. From students in our classrooms, to actors and writers on our stage, to the audiences in our seats, the BNW and all who have worked there have been able to create and recreate viable productions without compromising our standards of intelligent, issue-based comedy. Now I'd like to share these secrets of our success with you.

I wrote this book to ensure that the wisdom, traditions, and processes established by the BNW will be recorded and preserved. As an improviser, I believe the next scene is a direct result of all the scenes that came before it. I feel it is time to give the idea generation process its due respect. I want to ensure that our innovative process continues to grow and evolve. The BNW adheres to the following secrets as much for profitability as for creative expression. Like any business, the theatre needs to ensure its continued existence by creating experiences and productions that guarantee audience excitement and loyalty. Relying on the principles included in this book, the theatre operates as one of only a few self-sustaining, nonprofit theatre organizations in the country; we do not rely on corporate or government grants or donations.

I wrote this book also because I have been asked to share the theatre's secrets of innovation. The idea generation process and secrets I reveal are applicable to any sketch writer, playwright, actor, director, or theatre administrator—whether working alone or as an ensemble—who needs to create or sharpen the next great idea. While I believe the path to each person's most creative self is unique for every individual, and therefore every organization, I hope this book gives you better perspective, and perhaps more insight, into your own innovative path. Perhaps something within these pages will create an "aha" moment—a breakthrough that leads to greater confidence in and comfort with your own creative self. On a daily basis, BNW improvisation students and BNW employees have these "aha" moments—they stumble upon, or discover, or accidentally come up with wonderful, creative ideas. As students and staff are exposed to these secrets, they can clearly identify an increase in their innovative productivity. I sincerely hope this book helps you with that same transformation.

I also hope this book will draw attention to the Brave New Workshop Theatre and honor its founder, Dudley Riggs. For nearly five decades, this magical comedy-theatre remained relatively unknown because Dudley adopted a truly Minnesotan lifestyle. He did not need to let the world know about his little theatre, let alone brag about the wonderful work the staff and casts created or the famous alumni they trained. Ridiculously successful individuals like Al Franken (author/performer/activist), Mo Collins (writer/performer—*Mad TV*), Tom Sherohman (writer—*Mr. Magoo, Change of Seasons*), Peter Tolan (writer/producer—*The Larry Sanders Show, Murphy Brown, Analyze This*), Pat Proft (writer—*Scary Movie 3, The Naked Gun*), Irv Letofsky (theatre critic—*Los Angeles Times*), Linda Wallem (writer/producer—*That '70s Show*), Peter MacNicol (actor—*Sophie's Choice, Ally McBeal*), Mike McManus (writer—*M.A.S.H.*), Nancy Steen (head writer—*Happy Days*), Melissa Peterman (costar—*Reba*), Cedric Yarbrough (actor—*Reno 911!*), and countless others have all learned the following secrets and honed their skills on BNW stages.

Creating improvisation and sketch comedy is just a small portion of what the BNW has accomplished. We have taken the innovation process outside the theatre and developed products for other companies. This "corporate" line of services has been a wonderful byproduct of a rich comedic tradition and is currently the fastest-growing part of the BNW business. Because so many people have asked BNW staff and cast to share what they know, we have found ourselves in vastly varied and wonderfully uncommon situations to which we can contribute.

Like an ongoing improvisational scene, the BNW truly is the product of continuous innovation and hard work. Because we are able to consistently reinvent our products and ourselves, the BNW brand has become synonymous with quality satirical theatre. Our success is clearly the result of *all* of the people who have worked here and contributed to the "scene." Thousands of people have given small and large chunks of their lives to help this theatre adhere to its motto of "Promiscuous Hostility, Positive Neutrality." Some of them gave hours, others gave years, some gave decades, and a couple of them were actually paid.

There is no magic pill, a single event, or even a book that will instantly give you more creativity and innovation. But if you embrace these secrets we share and if you utilize our process, you can enhance your creativity and realize your artistic goals.

What is Improvisation?

There are hundreds of definitions of improvisation, and numerous books have been written about the topic. For our purposes, I will focus on the Brave New Workshop's definition—the one that has driven our company for all these years and will continue to do so.

First, it's important to know that our definition is borne from the firm belief that absolutely anyone can improvise if they allow themselves to play. For every person who has entered the doors of our theatre, has trained in our improv classes, has participated in one of our corporate services events, or even has laughed as part of our theatre audience, we believe the art of improvisation can help every individual find his/her most creative and innovative self.

At the BNW, we define improvisation as "an attitude that allows one person, or a group of people, to innovate and create instantly by using their own sense of trust, truth, acceptance, and creativity." Pure improvisation can happen only when the group works as a team and ideas and actions flow freely without judgment. Improvisation is NOT about being the quickest, smartest, or funniest, or about being "right."

Improvisation is a powerful tool for all theatre professionals; it can help the sketch writer or the playwright, the actor or the director to see his/her sketch, play, or character in a new light, opening up all sorts of creative possibilities and innovations, and infusing the project with a unique light. When improvisation works, it is magical, powerful, and undeniably effective as a source of creative inspiration and fuel.

The History of Improvisation

There are many versions of the history of improvisational theatre. Each version cites slightly different origins. There are a few people, however, who are synonymous with its creation, including Viola Spolin, Dudley Riggs, Paul Sills, Del Close, David Shepherd, and Keith Johnstone. In addition, there were probably several others who explored unique ways of interacting with audiences, not unlike theatrical improvisation, and I apologize to them for not knowing who they are. The following timeline highlights some of the most widely recognized contributors to modern-day improvisation and should give you a taste for how the art form developed.

1500s *Europe*	Nearly all histories of improvisation mention commedia dell'arte as the oldest ancestor to modern-day improvisation. In Europe, commedia dell'arte featured traveling entertainers who performed entirely improvised dialogue within a scene.
1933 *Chicago*	Viola Spolin develops a new style of instruction based on the belief that children would be more likely to enjoy acting classes if the main points were learned through games. Her son, Paul Sills, continues his mother's work at the University of Chicago in the mid-1950s. He later works with Del Close and David Shepherd (see 1955 below).
1946 *Hollywood*	Spolin creates the Young Actor's Company.
1952 *New York City*	Dudley Riggs founds the Instant Theatre Company, based on the comedy of vaudeville. As part of its growth, the troupe begins asking audiences for suggestions during performances. In 1959 the Instant Theatre Company makes its way to Minneapolis, and in 1961 it is renamed the Brave New Workshop. The theatre soon becomes home to improvisation in the Twin Cities. It remains one of the few satirical comedy theatres in the country.
1955 *Chicago*	Del Close and David Shepherd work with Sills to create an ensemble acting-troupe to appeal to the average Joe. The group they form is called the Compass Players. In 1959 this group shapes the foundation of Second City, a famous improv ensemble still in existence today.
1960 *Multiple locations*	A spin-off of the Compass Players, the Premise opens in New York, Washington, and London; it closes in 1963.

1963 *California*	Improv group the Committee is formed in Los Angeles and San Francisco; it gives birth to a variety of companies that succeed it.
1965 *Delano,* *California*	Cesar Chavez and playwright Luis Valdez organize farm workers into a theatre, El Teatro Campesino (The Farmworkers Theatre), which in 1968 becomes a theatre in its own right. In 1971, El Teatro Campesino relocates to San Juan Bautista. The troupe is credited with creating teatro chicano, a form of theatre that includes elements of commedia dell'arte.
Late 1960s, early 1970s *Canada*	Keith Johnstone, then teaching at the University of Calgary, combines the work of Viola Spolin with elements of sports to develop a unique form of improvisation—Theatresports. Over the next several years, leagues develop across Canada, the United States, and elsewhere.
1968 *New York*	Improv group the Fourth Wall plays for a couple of years in New York City.
1969 *Boston*	Improv group the Proposition begins; it continues today.
1975 *Los Angeles*	Improv group Off the Wall plays until 1999.
1976 *Los Angeles*	Improv group the Groundlings begins productions; they remain active today.
1976 *Los Angeles*	Improv group War Babies opens, but closes in 1986.
1981 *Chicago*	ImprovOlympic is formed by Charna Halpern; it is still operating today.
1984 *Los Angeles*	Improv group the Wims starts (and stops) playing.
Present	There are thousands of improvisation groups around the globe!

One of the common characteristics of improv theatres is a short lifespan. It is one of the reasons I feel so strongly about sharing the Brave New Workshop's creative process. Dudley Riggs's humble humor, keen satirical insight, boundless creativity, and circus-bred spontaneity have kept the theatre running for more than forty-five years and are the foundation of his legacy, on which we continue to build.

Part 2

The 8 Secrets of BNW Creativity

We believe that the following eight secrets can help everyone within a theatre organization create better theatre—from the writer to the actor to the director to the administrator. Whether you are seeking to improve your sketch-writing skills, hone your organizational skills, increase your spontaneity and innovation, renew your insight and creative prowess, or even simply to dream up new venues to keep your theatre alive, these secrets can help. They have helped the Brave New Workshop to continually produce shows that meet our high artistic standards, that breach the cutting edge of comedy, and that our audiences love; they have helped spawn the careers of hundreds of Hollywood actors and writers; and they have helped keep the BNW financially afloat in a perilous artistic sea. We cling to these secrets because, in short, they work.

Following each secret, we've included several interactive exercises to help you learn by experience to put the secret into practice. We believe there are limitless ways to do improvisation exercises and we encourage you to make modifications to our exercises to suit your individual or group needs. Following each set of exercises, we provide insights that detail some of the things we've learned from doing these exercises and, again, we encourage you to keep notes of your own insights. The BNW feels it's disrespectful to the creative and improvisational spirit to assume there is only one way to do something—always being open to new and surprising discoveries is one sign of a pure improviser!

Secret 1
Accept All Ideas

Most often when people hear me talk about accepting all ideas, they assume I mean to accept ideas that they understand, are comfortable with, or that seem to make sense. In actuality, I really do mean *all* ideas—perhaps most importantly, the very ideas that you *don't* understand and *aren't* familiar with and that make you uncomfortable or that seem ridiculous or illogical. Remember, if the idea seems odd to you, most likely it seems normal to someone else, and vice versa.

Improvisers accept all ideas as gifts. Not having an idea or "gift" at the beginning of an improvisational scene leaves you alone onstage, in front of hundreds of people who have paid $22 to come see you be funny. Not being able to find the next funny thing to say or do is one of the most humbling and horrible experiences a person can have. I personally begin to hear the individual heartbeats of each audience member. I often hear my father's voice reminding me I should have stayed in real estate. At this point, if a fellow improviser enters the scene with an idea—any idea—it feels as if I have been thrown a life preserver, or in improv terminology, I've been given a gift. As you can imagine, in this situation I am never overcome with the need to judge that idea; I am grateful for it and accept it immediately. The challenge is to be able to treat ideas with the same level of gratefulness and acceptance when we are not in a situation of need.

Within the BNW idea generation process, I have found that accepting ideas not only demonstrates respect for the idea, it also demonstrates respect for the person who generated it. Conversely, when someone negates an idea, they almost always indirectly negate the individual who presented the idea.

In terms of productivity, a consistent and clear acceptance of people's ideas creates the expectation that their ideas will be met with a positive reaction, rather than disagreement or judgment. As a result, people tend to increase the number of ideas they produce, and consequently the quality of the script or scene. As proven time and time again, from Pavlov's dogs to child development, positive reinforcement elicits a faster rate of learning and a quicker response to consistent stimuli.

I find that when the status quo of the environment is to accept *all* ideas, people become accustomed to the positive reinforcement and respond by producing more, and better, ideas in order to recreate the positive experience. If a person is used to—or, worse yet, *expects*—their idea will likely be rejected, they have a tendency to create fewer ideas in order to minimize the occurrences of negative experiences. There is a huge difference between *accepting* someone's idea and actually executing it. Most individuals are much more interested in having their ideas heard and respected than in having them implemented. Accepting an idea simply lets a person know you heard them and that you will treat their idea as a valid possibility.

A typical improv scene lasts between two and three minutes long. Within that time frame, improvisers must work together as a team in order to figure out and declare who they are, where they are, and what they want to accomplish. They must define and distribute individual roles, create some comedic conflict, and resolve the scene. They must do all of this based on a random suggestion from the audience, who expects the improvised scene to be hilarious. Due to the inherent speed and pressure of this process, improvisers have learned (over many years) that if a cast member chooses not to accept an idea, huge amounts of precious time are wasted, and the scene stops moving forward toward a successful solution.

I have to admit that at times I become cynical and almost want to believe it is human nature *not* to accept the ideas of others. I find that the skill of accepting all ideas is perhaps one of the hardest to teach to both improvisers and other professionals. I am reminded of our tendency to disagree when I witness improvisers passionately arguing about whose made-up idea is right or wrong. Although nothing that an improviser does exists within "the real world," we still find the need to defend our imagination and to disagree with the imaginations of others. Some of these arguments, in which the subject matter is make-believe, are as humorous as the scenes we perform.

I remember during the course of one BNW show, an actor came forward miming as if she were holding a large fish. The piano player started to play music from the movie *Jaws*. The actor holding the fish literally stopped the scene and glared at the piano player. Instantly, the stage was filled with an awkward sense of confusion. Another actor had to stop the scene and start a new one. During the post-show discussion, when we were critiquing each other's work and evaluating our performance, the piano player asked why the actor had reacted so strongly to his musical response. The actor who had mimed holding the fish was still angry and pointed out that earlier in the scene she had clearly "set the scene" in a freshwater environment. It was therefore "wrong" for the piano player to inaccurately decide that the fish she was holding was a shark (the actor falsely believed sharks were exclusively salt-water inhabitants—an assumption that was corrected by a third cast member, from New Zealand, who pointed out that there are in fact freshwater sharks). How typical of human nature to contradict others' ideas even when the basis of the contradiction is about a completely fictitious subject matter.

Most of the memorable, best-improvised scenes of which I have been a part started with ideas I did not understand, was not comfortable with, or considered atypical or illogical. Yet these scenes stand out in my mind as being incredibly successful, undeniably funny, vivid examples of what can happen when we accept all ideas.

An Exercise to Learn By
Everybody Go

The group forms a circle. One member begins by stepping forward and saying "everybody go _____" and proceeds to perform a physical action and/or to make a sound. The group then responds in unison by saying "yes!" and proceeds to mimic the exact sound and/or movement that the individual just declared. Each member takes a turn as the leader, and each member is met with an unconditional and enthusiastic "yes!" by the group. If done in a playful, open, accepting manner, this exercise immediately creates a safe, trusting environment for the group, in which all *ideas are clearly accepted.*

Insights

1. Each idea presented must immediately be met with a resounding "yes!" in order to truly build individual and group confidence. The more each group member hears "yes!" (and the more each member says "yes!"), the more likely it is that members will instinctually accept all ideas as a practice. Just one hesitation by the group will breed a sense of fear and judgment, as group members might think, "well, we're supposed to say yes, but I guess that's only if the idea is good and everyone understands it."
2. Practice immediately accepting the leader's idea (with a "yes!" and by instantly replaying the physical activity and sound), regardless of your own comfort level with that activity and sound. By offering an immediate supportive response, you train yourself to accept without question (which will keep you open to more and more ideas). Saying "yes!" first also holds your critical voice at bay until it is needed—later, if ever.
3. Another way to expand on this exercise is to have group members not only say "yes!" and repeat the leader's idea, but also to have members "heighten" the leader's idea when they repeat it. These actions show the leader that you respect his/her idea enough to not only repeat it but to "repeat it bigger, more intensely, and with added commitment." Make sure you are truly repeating and respecting the leader's idea when you heighten, rather than "changing" the leader's idea. There is a difference. One shows honor and acceptance for the leader's idea, and the other says, "well, yeah, I saw what you did, but I think I'll do it my way." To truly accept all ideas, you have to pay attention and listen, so you can receive the other person's idea, not your own version of their idea.
4. Even though the rule for this exercise states that everyone must say "yes!" to all ideas, no matter what, it is inevitable that some group members will still judge their own ideas. A participant will likely hear their own judging voice tell them, "well, they are saying yes to everyone's ideas, but my idea is stupid and they'll probably hate it," or "I can't think of anything 'good' to say or do. This is going to be embarrassing." Accepting all ideas has to begin with the acceptance of our own ideas. In fact, sometimes saying "yes!"

to our own ideas is much more difficult (and scary) than accepting other's ideas.

Another Exercise to Learn By
What Are You Doing?

Players form one line. One player jumps forward to begin this exercise, and begins a motion/activity suggested by the facilitator or by the group (for example, "brushing your teeth"). The player then immediately begins physically acting as if s/he is brushing his/her teeth. After a few moments, the first person in the line steps forward and says to the person brushing his/her teeth, "What are you doing?" The person acting the motion immediately responds, "I'm brushing my teeth," and then states another activity completely unlike the one s/he is currently doing (for example, "juggling bowling balls"). The person who was brushing teeth goes to the end of the line. The person who was first in line and who first asked "What are you doing?" then immediately jumps forward and begins "juggling bowling balls." This pattern continues with each new person in line asking, "What are you doing?" and each person who is acting out an activity suggesting a new activity. Players must accept their partner's idea immediately and quickly jump in and do the activity suggested. The person acting out the activity should also accept their own ideas and instincts about how to do the activity, with little thought. There is no wrong way to act out the activity as long as the player accepts the idea, jumps in, and quickly commits to the activity.

Insights

1. This game is usually played at a quick, physical pace, which will force players to immediately jump in and accept all ideas, without time to judge. The physical element of this game will also help players stay "out of their heads" and will help them just jump in and be accepting. By starting something without much thought, players have no choice but to accept the idea that was given. And

by physically moving their bodies in a positive manner, the players' minds will follow.
2. Group members should play, have fun, commit, jump in, accept, and just generally go for it. The more fun they are having, the more physical they are, the more they just jump in and try something, the easier it will be for players to accept all ideas, no matter what.
3. Help group members avoid stalling. It will be easy for players to accept the idea if it seems easy to do, is familiar, or doesn't involve embarrassment. It's the unusual, scary, or unfamiliar ideas that will sometimes stump a player and put them in a place of fear, making them stop, hesitate, or not accept the idea. Remind players that this is improvisation. No matter what a player's partner suggests (whether it's "brush your teeth," "recite a poem in Spanish," or "build a nuclear bomb"), the player should just jump in, accept the idea, and do something. There is no wrong way to do it because it is improvisation and the player's version of a Spanish poem or nuclear bomb will be as real and as good as any other version. It does not have to be correct or accurate. It just has to be committed and accepted and done. In fact, when players automatically accept ideas they don't understand and go forward anyway, it is a brave, wonderful, improvisational thing to do. Encourage everyone to do it and make sure you create a safe environment so they can do it. If someone gets the suggestion to "recite a poem in Spanish," and that person knows nothing about Spanish or poetry, if s/he innocently jumps in and begins humming some gibberish while dancing around the room, the group has to support that player and his/her instinct to accept the assignment no matter what.
4. Accepting the seemingly unacceptable opens up a multitude of creative possibilities. Saying yes to ideas that seem different or odd or scary gives a player a creative edge. This player will travel where many others won't . . . where many others would stop, this player will go. The player's partner may suggest the activity "eat live worms" or something equally grotesque or impossible, to which many people would have an immediate negative reaction, refusing to accept the activity. But a player who accepts such an activity, and who really goes for it, will discover something new

and creative, and sometimes even something funny. Jumping in and doing the activity suggested, no matter what, puts a player in a place where anything is creatively possible. What a wonderful, powerful, grand place to be!
5. As in any improvisation exercise, remind players not to think ahead when they are waiting in line. They will come up with an idea when they need to, in that moment. It will be perfect and great. They do not need to think ahead about what activity they will suggest, as that would pull them out of the moment and put them in the frame of mind that there are ideas that are good and ideas that aren't so good. Remember, it is important to accept *all* ideas. All ideas have pure potential.
6. The more physical, more committed, and more fun the players add to this game, the greater strides they will make in learning to accept all ideas no matter what. By having fun and fully engaging our physical bodies, our minds and souls will follow.

Secret 2
Defer Judgment

In order to create our shows and to improvise, BNW staff and actors consistently utilize the skill of deferring judgment. If there is one thing our theatre has learned in over forty-five years of producing innovative sketch comedy, it is that at the beginning of the idea generation process, quantity is much more important than quality. As you will find when you read about our funnel process later in this book, we create approximately 600 one-sentence ideas in order to produce the twenty-five sketches or songs that ultimately represent the finished show. We completely defer judgment during the first 15 percent of our idea generation process in order to enable us to produce the bulk of ideas we need in order to "fill the pot."

Our ability to defer judgment is based on the understanding that we need *all* 600 ideas in order to produce a few implementable ones. Many times the ideas we actually implement come as a result of combining or integrating several ideas. These ideas sometimes bear little resemblance to the original idea.

As a group, we understand that early in the idea generation process our goal is not to come up with "the" idea but to come up with "an" idea. This understanding allows us to rapidly produce mass quantities of ideas and it reduces the time constraints and fear involved in self-editing and judgment.

To encourage judgment deferral, we practice a recognition policy that rewards cast members for the number of ideas they produce, not the quality of those ideas. Our goal is to become "idea machines." To increase the efficiency and production pace of these "machines," the obstacle of judgment needs to be eliminated.

Cast members must also trust that the process and hard realities of implementation will judge the idea and determine its validity. We recognize and are fully aware of the fact that all ideas will be judged and refined based on budget, physical theatre restrictions, the actors' individual abilities, marketability, and the like. Since these judgments are inevitable, we do not concern ourselves with them at this point. We simply produce ideas regardless of how the idea may or may not ultimately work due to outside restrictions, which saves a lot of time in the long run. By deferring judgment, we can focus entirely on the production of ideas and not be distracted by details that may or may not come into play at a later date.

By treating judgment deferral almost as a policy, our cast members, especially those motivated by doing things the "right way," feel comfortable learning and practicing a skill that is different and sometimes even in contrast to typical or standard creative practices. The policy of deferring judgment also helps individuals unlearn the seemingly automatic response of "what's wrong with that idea is" or "the reason that won't work is."

Because the accepted group-standard is to defer judgment and because BNW management clearly sets the expectation that judgment deferral is required, an individual exhibiting judgment clearly stands out as someone who is not participating well in the process. This sort of group-behavior observation and playful peer pressure creates an environment in which the only way an individual can screw up is to judge.

Another tool we use to maximize this part of the idea generation process, and therein the quality of our ultimate show, is to require the group to generate a set minimum number of ideas before they are allowed to move on to the next step. Over the years, we have determined that, for the creation of our show scripts, that minimum number of ideas is about 600. This tactic prevents the group from worrying about the next step and allows them to focus solely on the task at hand—idea generation with reckless abandon.

An Exercise to Learn By

What's in the Box?

Group members form two lines facing each other. The first person in one line approaches the first person in the other line and hands him/her an imaginary box. The receiver of the box says "Thank you" (make them say thank you as another way to train group members to always, always respond positively first) and then asks, "What's in the box?" The giver responds by telling the receiver what is in the box (an alligator, a diamond, a dirty sock; anything that comes to mind is fine—there is no right or wrong reply). The receiver responds positively by saying, for example, "Thank you for this alligator. This alligator is the perfect gift for me because I have a swamp in my yard that needs some life" or "Wonderful! I really could use an alligator because my watchdog died last week."

The two group members who have been interacting now go to the ends of the opposite lines and the next two members in line repeat the exercise. The idea of this exchange is that no matter what "gift" is given in the imaginary box, the receiver defers all judgment and gratefully accepts the gift, acknowledging that s/he has a specific use for that gift. Frequently our first response to an idea (or gift, for that matter) is to judge or critique it—an action that not only brings the creative process to a screeching halt but also insults the idea giver (and ensures that s/he will be a bit more fearful when offering his/her next idea). This exercise makes members practice judgment deferral by assuming all gifts are useful and full of pure potential.

Insights

1. How many times do we charge ahead and forget to say "thank you"? While it may seem simplistic or repetitive, actually saying "thank you" is so important; it communicates that you've heard the idea, accept the idea, are honored to have received the idea, and are grateful to get the idea. Saying "thank you" also forces players to be positive first, which will make them less likely to "judge" the idea.
2. After the group has become practiced at accepting each other's ideas as gifts, try the following adjustment to the exercise: Instruct the gift-givers to intentionally give gifts they think the receiver would not want or would dislike. Instruct the receiver that, no matter what gift they receive, they still need to immediately reply with a thank you and a positive response. This adjustment challenges the receiver to truly defer judgment and to accept all ideas as positive contributions to the creative process. For example, if the gift-giver presents an imaginary box containing a dozen moldy socks, the receiver's reaction should be "thank you" followed by a reason they could use some moldy socks. Our first gut reaction to a gift like this would probably be "yuck, I don't want moldy socks," which immediately eliminates any possibility of going forward with this unusual and perhaps brilliant idea. As improvisers, we believe that any and all ideas have positive value. This adjustment to the game really challenges the group's instinct to judge first.
3. When participants are giving and receiving gifts in this game, make sure they face each other and make eye contact throughout the entire exercise. Sometimes a group member will give his/her gift and then, in a moment of relief, walk away before receiving a thank you from his/her partner. It is not uncommon during improvisation exercises for players to get nervous or excited and walk away before the exercise is complete. It is important, however, to remind players that they are working within a group and that listening and receiving are as vital as speaking and giving.
4. As with all improvisation-based exercises, encourage group members to avoid planning their ideas and gifts ahead of time. Oftentimes, players will be waiting in line or waiting their turn and what

is running through their head is: "What gift am I going to give?" "Will it be stupid?" "I can't think of anything," etc. While it might initially be scary for group members, they should practice *not* planning ahead by waiting until they jump to the front of the line to discover their idea. Then they should accept and give the first idea that comes to them. In this way they are also practicing judgment deferral (and accepting all ideas) with their own ideas. Also, if they are thinking ahead while they are waiting in line, they are not paying attention to their classmates who are at the front of the line. Finally, thinking ahead and trying to plan the "right" gift only fosters judgment and critical thinking in our sneaky brains. We are trying to "defer" judgment, accept ideas, and play.

Another Exercise to Learn By
Sound and Motion Circle

The group stands in a circle. One person is chosen to begin the exercise, and starts by turning to the person next to him/her and delivering a simultaneous sound and motion. The person receiving the sound and motion observes closely (and quickly), then immediately mimics the exact sound and motion and sends it off to the next person in the circle. That person receives it and quickly sends it along to the next person in the circle, and so on. The sound and motion continues quickly traveling around the circle as each group member receives it and sends it along.

This exercise is sort of a physical version of the old telephone game. When beginning this exercise, instruct players to really try to accept and mimic exactly what's given to them, instead of trying to change it. As the sound and motion travels around the circle, guide the group to let the energy flow very quickly. In this way, players must keep the pace going and do not have time to judge or to change the flow. There are many variations that can be played and discovered, all encouraging players not to judge or control the energy but simply to allow the energy to flow freely.

Insights

1. When players are physically engaged, are playful, and are in the flow, it is much easier to defer judgment. Judgment often comes into play when our bodies and/or our minds are idle, waiting nervously for the next thing to happen or the next brilliant idea to hit us. When we're in this idle mode, fear is often the first visitor to our minds and bodies, and fear breeds judgment. This game forces players to defer judgment because they are so fully engaged in the flow that they do not have time to judge. By practicing this automatic deferment of judgment, players build confidence and trust; they learn they don't have to try to control things but can instead simply play with what is given to them and make that work.

2. Judgment stops all flow. If someone judges in this game, it will literally stop the energy and motion dead in its tracks. A facilitator can step outside the circle to observe and to help the group if they fall into judging traps. It may be as obvious as someone receiving a sound and motion and then sending a completely different sound and motion to the next person. It will feel like someone just pushed the skip button on the CD player—an abrupt, out-of-left-field shift in the energy. Or it might be more subtle, like someone changing the sound and motion given to them by putting a "better" spin on it. In either case, a player has felt the need to change the flow, as if it were not good enough or because it was not to his/her liking. The player judged what was happening in the circle and felt compelled to fix it. Remind players that the flow, energy, sound, and motion are just what they are. Trying to figure it out, change it, make it better, or make it funnier are all versions of "judging" that will change the group flow of the circle.

3. When players are in the circle waiting their turn, sometimes idleness will invite judgment to creep in. A player might be watching the sound and motion travel around the circle and think, "that person didn't do that right" or "I don't like that motion; I hope it changes before it gets to me" or "I can't do that; that's stupid." Sometime a player will watch the sound and motion as it approaches and will mimic the sound and motion that was sent two or three people before him/her. In this way, the player was

anticipating what might be coming and was judging what might be coming but didn't stay fully in the moment to accept what was actually given to them. Encourage players to defer judgment at *all* times during this game, not just when it's their turn. While they are waiting, they can be watching their fellow players and simply enjoying the goofiness and fun of the game. Simply watch, stay focused, and only when it is your turn should you jump in and go along with what is given. It will be easier if the group plays quickly and effortlessly. When players are not judging and are playing freely, the group will be rewarded with a fast, easy, fun, entertaining energy; it will feel as if the exercise has a life of its own, a bit like hopping on a carnival ride and letting go.

4. Even when players are doing a great job of really paying attention and mimicking exactly what they are given, the facilitator will observe that the sound and motion organically changes and morphs. This happens because of the subtle (or not so subtle) differences in the players' voices and bodies, proving that when a group works as a team and is truly connected to the group flow, there is no need for judgment or control. There is no need for someone to take charge and change the sound just because they think it needs to change; it will happen on its own because of the group flow. If judgment is brought in, it will reflect one person's need to control instead of the group's organic improvisational energy.

5. If the group seems to be flowing well, without judgment, there is another variation of this game that can be tried. When a player receives the sound and motion, s/he immediately should accept it without judgment, mimic it, and also heighten it. Be careful that players are not changing the sound and motion, but are really accepting what is given and just doing "more of it." In so doing, players are not only deferring judgment but are honoring the idea given to them by committing even more energy to it. The sound and motion will travel around the circle and will organically morph and change a bit more quickly, but will still have a fluid, continuous feel to it. The same guidelines apply, however, to keep players from trying to stop, judge, or change the flow.

Secret 3
Share Focus & Accept All Styles

Because the actors of the Brave New Workshop are also improvisers, they have an inherent ability to share focus with each other on stage. As an improv scene progresses, the actors organically decide to react in a way that gives the appropriate person the proper amount of focus at any given time during the scene. They change their position on stage so that the person speaking can be most clearly seen by the audience and they create a seamless "give and take" in their dialogue to ensure that two people are not speaking at the same time. To the audience it appears as if the actors have a set discipline or that the scene is in fact scripted and rehearsed. The truth is, the actors are simply respectful of each other's need for focus and they put the success of the scene ahead of their own need to have their ideas heard. Unlike stand-up comedy, improvisation actually rewards the performers for a sense of egoless cooperation.

Improvisers also understand that respecting drastically different styles is a way to add depth and dimension to the scene. Two characters with significantly different points of view and different styles can create a much more richly entertaining scene than two similar characters. There are countless examples of this in well-known comedies; for example, Archie Bunker and Meathead in *All in the Family*, Frank Burns and Hawkeye in *M.A.S.H.*, Kramer and Jerry in *Seinfeld*, or Lisa and Bart Simpson in *The Simpsons*.

By accepting another person's unique style, you also show them they have your endorsement to be their most unique and original self. We have found this empowerment leads people to blossom and it increases their confidence and productivity. We have also observed that an ensemble made up of a diverse cast of characters generates shows that are consistently more innovative than a group made up of similar styles.

Accepting someone's style can be as easy as allowing them to communicate in the way in which they are most comfortable. Some people prefer written communication while others prefer verbal communication. Some people are more comfortable sharing their ideas one-on-one while others like the group dynamic.

Because our goal is to encourage everyone and to facilitate the blossoming of each individual's most original and unique self, it is vital that we allow each person to add to the process in his/her own way. We have found that the number of ideas a person can generate is directly related to his/her ability to communicate those ideas in a style with which s/he is most confident.

At first, many people think our concept of sharing focus means making sure that each individual gets their fifteen minutes on stage or that everyone gets equal time to communicate ideas within our creative process. However, this assumes everyone has similar needs and a similar level of comfort being the focus of attention. In fact, some individuals actually feel uncomfortable in the spotlight. We must give these individuals the opportunity to share ideas in the time they need and through the vehicle that works best for them. We have learned that, for many people, sharing ideas is a risk—especially if emotional consequences are attached to that sharing. If someone is fearful of the idea-sharing process, we work to create a mechanism that best suits his/her personality and style. Everyone is still responsible for equal portions of idea generation; however, they are allowed to meet their idea quota in a manner that maximizes their own preferred style of contribution.

By encouraging people to share ideas and focus in their own way, we have time after time found wonderful solutions from the ideas these nontraditional team members generate. Our shows have greatly benefited from some outlandish and innovative ideas that were a direct result of the manner in which the ideas were communicated to the rest of the group. In fact, the communication vehicle itself oftentimes was so unusual that it ended up in the show too. For example, during the writing process of one of our holiday shows, one of the actresses thought she could best communicate her idea by drawing kindergarten-style images with crayons on a piece of cardboard. That communication style ultimately inspired a sketch that featured a young foreign exchange student using crayon drawings to satirize her perception of the "American Christmas."

An Exercise to Learn By
Walk in Space

We start this exercise by asking all individual members of the group to begin randomly walking around in the space. The director then asks the group to freeze. One person (either randomly or as chosen by the director) creates a repetitive sound and motion and continues performing them while the other group members are still frozen. The person doing the sound and motion has the "focus" in the space. This person will continue to have the focus (by repeating the sound and motion) until s/he gives the focus to one of the frozen members in the group. The person may hand-off the focus via a simple gesture, eye contact, a tap to the shoulder, or any other method that signals a switch in focus. The person handing-off the focus immediately freezes as the new person receiving the focus starts a new repetitive sound and motion. Players continue sharing focus in this manner.

The object of this exercise is for the group to practice organically sharing focus with one another without having to plan ahead and without an assigned leader. The group should be able to take turns, share focus, and find a natural flow in this game, which creates a true sense of trust and sharing. You can vary the game by having the person in focus keep the focus until someone else in the group takes over the focus (i.e., the person in focus continues his/her sound and motion until someone else in the group randomly starts a new sound and motion). Or try a combination of both (i.e., sometimes focus is given and sometimes focus is taken).

Insights

1. Through this exercise, players learn about their own comforts (and discomforts) with having the group focused on them, with taking away the focus from another member, and with giving away the focus to another member. It is natural for some players to be more comfortable watching, while others are more comfortable in the spotlight. Remind players that they are a group and that the group

needs many different styles in order to be dynamic, complete, and creative, so there is no one style that is "better than" another style. The point is for the group to work together sharing the space, the air, and the energy, giving all members a chance to participate in their own way.

2. One way to ensure that group members are sharing focus and accepting each other's styles is to remind players that when they are frozen they should be listening to and giving their attention to the player in focus (rather than thinking ahead about what they might do when they get focus). If players are "in their heads" thinking about what they should do when it's their turn, they are not connected to the group process, they do not trust themselves, and they are going to miss valuable information and inspiration being delivered by other players. Also, if players are in their own heads they are not sharing focus, because they are trying to control the group or at least trying to control their little piece of the group. If this happens, the player is often simply nervous and does not trust that s/he will be able to do something "of value" when his/her turn arrives. Or sometimes the player does not trust that the process can work without some sort of master controller at the wheel so s/he feels the need to direct the outcome. In any case, remind players there is no judgment, there is no need to "be funny," there is no expectation that any of the sounds or motions make sense, and that the true goal of this game is to simply "play" while sharing focus.

3. Fun, unusual, and creative things can happen when players truly let the flow of this game happen and when they can be playful and observant. If everyone is committed to sharing focus and to some honest give-and-take, sometimes a story develops. Even though players are just doing seemingly silly noises and motions, we see themes and storylines develop. When this happens organically, we know the group is somehow connected, paying attention to one another and responding to one another's sounds and motions. After a few attempts at this game, the facilitator may even ask the group to really concentrate on the person in focus, and when a player takes (or is given) focus, to respond or react spon-

taneously only to the person who had focus immediately before you. This keeps all of the members in the moment and helps them to practice accepting the styles and ideas of everyone in the group (because they must react to the person before them, no matter what, instead of selecting another player's idea that they liked or one that they thought of on their own).
4. Part of sharing focus is playing varying roles. In this exercise, members' roles shift in the moment and without notice. Players must immediately accept a new role. At any given time, some players are supporting characters while others are in the spotlight. Players must always be awake, aware, and ready to gladly accept a role and share the responsibility of the game.
5. Another variation of this game is to allow players to also use words and sentences as they perform their sounds and motions. This variation can be more challenging in that sometimes when logical words, thoughts, and sentences are involved, players get stuck in their heads trying to "think" of the right thing to do. There is value in doing the exercise both ways (with words or with no words allowed). Some players find that with words, they are more connected to the group, while others find that the words make it cumbersome. If you are allowing players to use words, remind them to really listen and respond to the player who goes before them.

Another Exercise to Learn By
Conducted Story
Several members of the group stand shoulder to shoulder in a line. Another member or a facilitator stands in front of the group. The players will be cooperatively telling a story as a group. In the game "One-Word Story," players tell a story in which each member contributes one word at a time. In this exercise, however, players may contribute several words at a time, or even full sentences. The facilitator "conducts" the story by pointing to the member who should be talking at any given moment. The facilitator might start by pointing to the players in order, or s/he may point randomly. The facilitator may point to any one player for

just a few words or for longer periods. Group members must listen very carefully to the story at all times so that when they are selected they can pick up exactly where the previous person left off. If group members share focus, listen, and accept the storyline of the members before them, their combined points of view and unique perspectives can create a richer, more unique story than one individual alone could have produced.

Insights

1. Some players do not trust that the group can share the responsibility of the story, so they feel the need to plan ahead or to try to force the story in some specific direction. Other players may judge the story while they're playing and may decide that the story needs some humor or something shocking to make it more interesting. The facilitator should point out to the group that in order to truly share focus and accept all ideas, players need to surrender control and let go of preconceived ideas of where the story should go. The facilitator can also try to be unpredictable in their conducting, which will keep the players on their toes, giving them no choice but to improvise.
2. Once group members get the hang of this exercise, the facilitator can further challenge them by letting them know s/he may cut them off mid-sentence or even mid-word. It will then be the job of the next person selected to finish the sentence or even to finish a cut-off word. Remind players that part of the fun of this game is that different players will have very different ideas about how to finish a sentence or word.
3. Some group members may try to think ahead of time of something funny or shocking, keeping this idea in their back pocket so that when they are selected they can smoothly throw it out as if they are the cleverest person in the group. Try to catch this if this happens and remind players that it is much more challenging, risky, fun, and creative to really let go of preconceived ideas and surrender to the story. The story (the group) comes first, not any individual player.

Secret 4

Declarations

A declaration can be a statement or an action that clearly communicates your point of view or your feelings on a particular subject or at a particular time. A declaration is a gift to your improvisation partners because it tells them a bit about you and it gives them something to which to respond.

Many improvisers feel the first five seconds are the most important part of an improv scene. Within those five seconds, the impetus for the scene is born and the chain of declaration-reaction-action begins. Ensemble improvisation requires participants to constantly gather information from each other and to instantaneously create something from nothing. Declaring a point of view is not only polite, it is vital in helping your fellow improvisers understand what your deal is. It gives others a clear understanding of who you are so they can discover who they are.

At the BNW, we ask our improvisers to declare their point of view loudly, clearly, and quickly. We recognize this declaration is the foundation needed to build the scene. If two improvisers begin a scene with clearly stated points of view, then the scene can simply and organically focus on the two points of view working together to create the action of the scene while sharing space and time. It is a beautiful and clear representation of perfect collaboration.

If the declaration is not clear at the beginning of a scene, the scene tends to hobble along without much progress. The audience may notice that the improvisers seem to have a hint of confusion in everything they do. Declarations build clarity, which lead to confidence and purpose in an improv scene. Sometimes it feels as if the declarations at the top of a scene are like marching papers. When an improviser understands his/her own point of view along with the points of view of his/her fellow improvisers, the scene seems easier to navigate and almost writes itself.

There are many classic examples of this in well-known comedy. We, as viewers, didn't care what Sam and Diane from *Cheers* were doing, as long as they were doing it while sticking to their identifiable points of view. Each of the three "stooges" had a very clear and identifiable point of view; it didn't matter to us whether they were painting a house or stopping a bank robbery or going fishing—we just wanted to see them stick to their points of view and interact with each other.

In Minnesota we suffer from what is referred to as "Minnesota Nice," and part of our culture believes that clearly and loudly declaring your point of view is a sign of arrogance or inappropriate outspokenness. Some people have a tendency to never let anyone else know how they truly feel. This is death for an improvisation scene and for any group creative project, for that matter. I refer to it as the Minnesota Norwegian Lutheran Verbal Square Dance. The truth is, the nicest or most polite thing you can do is to confidently declare your point of view at the top of the scene.

I believe that declaring your point of view early and strongly can be applied to any situation in which a group is trying to evaluate a scene or a show, to find direction. Clear declarations at the beginning of any creative project significantly add to the quality of the finished project. If a person decides to withhold his/her point of view or otherwise useful information until late in the rehearsal process, the group must backtrack in order to incorporate the new information into their show.

Our concept of sharing focus and accepting all styles has a direct application to making declarations. Individuals must be able to declare their points of view via the style and communication vehicle that works best for them. However, the individual is also responsible for contributing to the process *early on,* supporting the group by ensuring that s/he decisively declares a point of view.

An Exercise to Learn By
Declaration Lines

For this exercise, have group members form two lines. The first person in each line steps forward and the two players face one another. The facilitator announces a topic to the two players. It can be anything—from politics to weather to something silly or mundane. A player starts the exercise by making the following declaration to the other player (filling the blanks we've left here):

"[topic given by facilitator] makes me feel _____, and if it were up to me, I would _____." For example, "Snow makes me feel excited, and if it were up to me, I would have fresh snow falling every day in the winter." The player receiving the declaration then lets the other player know s/he heard his/her declaration, and adds his/her own declaration. For example: "Oh, you get excited when it snows. Well, I used to get excited about snow when I was a kid, but now that I have a bad back and don't like to shovel, seeing snow makes me feel tired."

To really embrace creative expression, we need to allow, accept, and celebrate all the varying points of view players can express. This exercise helps create an environment that encourages varying points of view while at the same time enabling players to practice expressing those points of view.

Insights

1. Encourage players to jump in quickly once they hear the topic and simply make the first strong declaration that comes to them. There is no right or wrong answer. Players are just learning to make statements and declarations about how they feel and about who they are. Encouraging players to jump in quickly helps them stay out of their heads and reminds them it is not about doing the "right" or "best" thing but simply about jumping in and improvising. If someone seems hesitant or even stumped, try having them literally jump forward (with their bodies in motion) and begin the sentence without even thinking. If they just begin the declaration, something will follow.
2. If someone makes a statement with which their partner strongly disagrees and the partner balks, remind the responder that it is still very important to let the person making the declaration know that they heard them and respect them, even if they don't agree. This can be as simple as just repeating what the person declared (i.e., "I hear that you love snow"). Whether players have the same or differing points of view is not important; simply respecting one another as creative people takes precedence.

3. Encourage players to be bold and to make strong statements. This exercise is just for fun and there is no way to screw up, so really help players go for it. Making strong, committed declarations helps the creative process because it gives clear information to everyone in the group (to which they can respond) and also gets everyone emotionally involved. When players are emotionally involved, they often find it much easier to play and to create, because they are open, awake, and on their toes.
4. This process reinforces the idea that we need clear, direct statements to move forward. Some players will hesitate because they believe it is rude to be so direct, or because they simply have never been so direct in their lives. It is important to impress upon players that improvisers and co-creators *need* directness; it is a gift that provides a clear path to the group! In order to foster trust among group members, all declarations need to be embraced and recognized in the moment, not as overarching truths but as contributions to the creative process.
5. There are dozens of variations to this exercise. You may remove the structure, just throw out a topic, and have players jump and declare instantaneously whatever comes to them first. For example, the topic is snow and a player quickly jumps in, flinging his/her arms in the air and screaming, "Ahhhh, I love snow, I love snow, I love snow. I get to go skiing!" Try requiring a physical element, so that when a player jumps forward to make a declaration, s/he must also do something with his/her body (i.e., make a physical declaration). This exercise can also been done without words, requiring players to communicate their points of view using only sounds and motions. These are just a few ideas. Just remember that players are learning about expressing and accepting varying points of view, so try to encourage and applaud *any* declaration that comes from an honest place. By honest place, we mean any declaration that is not contrived with some ulterior motive. For example, if a player standing in line decides ahead of time that s/he will jump like a chicken and make a funny gurgle noise when it is his/her turn, s/he is not coming from an honest place. But a player who gets to the front of the line and truly lets go and just declares what

comes to him/her in the moment should be applauded no matter what the declaration.

Another Exercise to Learn By
Line Word Ball
Players form two single-file lines, facing each other. Someone chooses a topic. The first person in one line begins walking toward the first person in the other line. When they meet, the first person hands the other person an imaginary ball, says a word, and then walks to the end of the opposite line. The player who received the ball then walks toward the first person in the other line, hands them an imaginary ball, says a different word, and walks to the end of the opposite line. This cycle continues quickly, with players handing-off words and going to the ends of opposite lines.

The topic is simply a jumping-off point, something to inspire the first word-giver. From there, the words can be anything inspired by the word or by the person giving the word. Encourage players to move quickly, so they are not stuck thinking of the "best" or "right" word. There is no best or right word, of course, just honest statements and reactions.

Insights
1. Be physical (move your body). Have fun. Make eye contact. Move quickly. All of these suggestions will keep players out of their heads so they stay connected to their partners and to the game.
2. While the group should work quickly, they cannot work so quickly that they ignore their partners. The player receiving the ball and the word must still take a moment to receive the ball, hear the word, and let the word sink in enough that they can go and give someone else the ball and a word.
3. Remind players that they should not be thinking ahead of what word they will give, but should instead be focused on the person with the ball. When their turn arrives, something will come to them, and if they listen to and accept the word given to them, they

will have some sort of reaction that will allow them to react and give a word and the ball to the next person. It is not about saying the "right" or "appropriate" word but instead about hearing and accepting your partner's declaration. Don't "do" anything; just receive and react!
4. Try these variations:
   a) Go super fast so that players truly cannot think and must react very quickly.
   b) Move in slow motion so that all physical motions, expressions, and words are drawn out and exaggerated.
   c) Instead of handing-off a word, try handing-off a sound that still communicates some sort of statement or declaration.
   d) Vary the ball too. For example, players still say a word or a sound but they hand-off some sort of object or thing they are inspired to give in place of a ball.

Another Exercise to Learn By
Pass the Clap

This is a focus game and a group warm-up that requires members to have a high level of concentration and patience. In a circle, one group member begins by engaging another member, through eye contact, to clap with him/her simultaneously. Without speaking, the two clap their hands at the same time. The person who accepted the clap from the first group member then turns to make eye contact with another group member and the two players clap together. This exchange continues as the group works together to create a smooth rhythm and flow that builds in speed and confidence. If everyone in the group is awake, connected, and concentrating, the group will eventually be able to do the clapping very quickly.

Insights

1. Many groups start out awkwardly, barely able to clap alone, let alone at the same time as another person. This is normal, because they are still in their heads trying to figure out the rules. As they

trust and let go, they will be able to loosen up. After they've tried it a few times, ask them for suggestions as to how they can find that trust and flow on their own. They likely will have some insights.
2. Remember that one of the overall goals of this exercise is to practice making and accepting declarations. This exercise is a very simple, physical manifestation of those skills. The person with the focus (about to send the clap) must, without speaking, clearly declare his/her intent so that the person who will join him/her knows s/he is being selected. This is simply done with eye contact but as the group goes faster, some members will get anxious or excited and will forget to make eye contact or will look at two people. The power of the declaration will be obvious at this point, as the rhythm and flow fail with hesitation and lack of clear communication. The person receiving the declaration (clap) also has a responsibility to let the sender know they are ready and willing to accept that declaration. Again, it may be simple when the game is moving slowly but it becomes more difficult as the speed increases. So rather than focusing on when their turns might come or on the increasing speed of the game, players should focus on being ready and available to receive a clap. Once received, they should be absolutely clear about who they are sending it to.
3. This game is about clear communication. One way to help members communicate clearly is to encourage them to use their bodies. If they simply use their eyes and hands, their communication will be subtle and confusing. If they are awake and playful and their bodies are engaged, involved, and expressive, they will help the flow immensely. This could mean pointing your whole body, not just your eyes, toward the person who is to receive the clap, or by exaggerating your motions, or any number of other limitless possibilities. Play with it, have fun, and see what happens.

Secret 5

Create a Statusless Environment

By watching thousands of improv scenes and by observing actors and writers create a show, I have witnessed how both perceived and actual levels of status can affect an individual's ability to freely create. As a company, the BNW has observed firsthand that if the levels of status can be flattened within a group, it generally increases the comfort level, openness, and productivity of the group. By adhering to our belief that all ideas are equal, we must also view the creators of the ideas as equal. Taking it a step further, we believe that everyone has the same creative potential, so it is easy for us to perceive all members of our theatre equally. We reinforce our theory of the statusless environment by aggressively involving people of differing experience levels in the idea generation process.

By its very nature, improvisation demands that status be eliminated. For instance, if a member of an improv scene decides that s/he has more, or less, status than the others in the group, our scene has a fundamental problem. An individual who decides to increase his/her status will gain control of the scene and move it in a predetermined personal direction—that's not improvisation. The progress of a scene is negatively affected when an individual centers on him- or herself, because very few actors can read minds. The team thus becomes paralyzed and is afraid to further the scene because they have no way of knowing or understanding what direction the "self-declared leader" has taken. Communication breaks down and confusion replaces creation for the remainder of the scene. The audience withdraws, sensing the scene has lost its natural progression and is no longer pure improvisation—unrehearsed and spontaneous. This dynamic of "leader-follower" moves the improv scene from an organic creative flow to a structured and awkward game of "Simon says, stand on your toes and twirl."

A common improvisational jargon term is "follow the follower"—meaning there is no leader and, at any given time, no *one* person is steering or dictating the direction of the scene. Within an improv scene, the organic flow of the scene determines the role of each actor. No one should ever feel obligated to lead the scene but instead should simply listen and follow the flow of the scene. Good improvisers understand and accept the role the scene requires and simply say yes to that role. If a group of improvisers performs ten successful scenes, each scene will naturally direct group members to take on different roles and to contribute differently each time.

It is important not to confuse status with personal focus or commitment to a scene. At any given moment, one person may seem to be the focal point or center of the scene. This isn't necessarily a reflection of status; it may simply be the role the scene is asking that person to fill. There is a difference between an organic response to what the scene needs and a manufactured status. Manufactured status is contrived, planned, or manipulated based on personal need for power, attention, or ego, while organic response is natural, free-flowing, and recognizably spontaneous.

An Exercise to Learn By
Pattern Game

The group forms a circle to do this pattern exercise, and will create two or three separate verbal patterns. To start, a category needs to be selected (e.g., types of fruit). If the category is fruit, then player 1 may say apple, player 2 say grape, player 3 say apricot, and so on until every member has said one fruit. Once each member has said one fruit name, then the group repeats the entire pattern, with each individual always saying the same fruit in the same order (i.e., player 1 always says apple, followed by player 2 saying grape, followed by player 3 saying apricot, etc.).

The group should not simply move in sequence around the circle to determine the order of who speaks when. For example, say there are five players, with Fred sitting next to Mary sitting next to Patty sitting next to Jeff sitting next to Ted. The pattern shouldn't simply pass from Fred to Mary to Patty to Jeff to Ted. Instead, the pattern may start with Fred and then go to Jeff and then to Mary and then to Ted and then to Patty, or some other variation. However, if Fred says "apple" the first time, he will say "apple" every time, and it will always be after Patty says "pear" and before Jeff says "apricot."

The group thus creates their first pattern (types of fruit), and, once they've repeated this pattern several times, they create a second pattern (e.g., names of cars). This second pattern should move in a different sequence. So, this time Ted will start the pattern and then it will move to Mary and then Patty and then Jeff and then Fred, or some other variation that differs from the one the group started with. Once the second pattern is created, the group should practice it a few times before moving on to the next step.

Now for the biggest challenge. Once two patterns have been created, the group should try to speak both patterns simultaneously, keeping both patterns going at the same time. So, while Fred is starting pattern 1 with "apple," Ted is starting pattern 2 with "Honda." Group members need to listen carefully to know when to say their "fruit" and when to say their "car."

This exercise is comparable to a group verbal-juggling game. If the group masters two patterns, a third can be attempted (or more, if the group is really good). Each group member must stay focused on his/her role in the game in order to ensure that the pattern continues without stopping.

Insights

1. Try the game a few times and see what goes well and what doesn't. Ask the players for comments and observations, and see if they can figure out how to work effectively. If a problem occurs, it is often very telling and will help teach the point of this exercise. The primary goal here is to illustrate that we each play an equal role in the group and if we try to do less or more than our role, the game will not work.
2. If players are really having difficulties (this exercise can be very difficult), instruct them to remember two things (if two patterns are going): the name of the fruit (or other item) before them, and the name of the car (or other item) before them. Ask them to really concentrate on only these two things; it will help them to focus on their role. When players instead, for example, try to remember everyone's fruit and car, they become a liability to the group. This exercise beautifully illustrates that when everyone maintains equal status and does only their part (without trying to control or manage everyone else), the group can accomplish seemingly impossible tasks.
3. In our lives (as workers, parents, friends, artists), we are constantly asked to multitask. Most of us have to juggle many relationships

and many tasks. If we look at our task list as a whole, it seems unmanageable and can make us scream with terror. But if we take the list piece by piece, we can manage just fine. This exercise helps us practice taking the process piece by piece, as the world is spinning quickly around us. In this game, it will feel like there are a dozen words being shouted out all at once. It will feel like things are moving too quickly. But if each member of the group focuses on just his/her task (just the fruit and the car before him/her), the pattern will flow seamlessly. This exercise requires trust and a commitment to statusless play.

Another Exercise to Learn By
Count to Ten

The group forms a circle and attempts to count to ten, one member at a time. This should be attempted without any predetermined order of who will say what number when. Anyone can begin and anyone can say the next number at any time, but if more than one person says a number at the same time, the group must start over from number one. This exercise requires patience, trust, and group focus. If the group reaches ten without two or more people speaking at once, see how much higher the group can go (fifteen? twenty? etc.).

Insights

1. Often players will try to figure out the "trick" or the "right way" to do this exercise. There is none. Even worse, sometimes a person in the group will try to tell the others how to do it or what to do next. This person perhaps does not believe in a statusless group environment and feels "there must be a leader or someone in charge—how else can we complete this task?" If this happens, it provides a beautiful illustration of the point of this exercise: There is no need for a leader, for rules, or for a method to get to ten. In fact, the more each person in the group releases the need to control and to "figure it out," the more likely the group will reach ten or higher.

2. During this game, sometimes players get nervous, thinking the game cannot be done, and they try to create rules. Sometimes they'll say things like, "Okay, if you are about to speak, nod your head" or "everyone has to say a number once." However, the group has to find their way to ten without any rules—that's the whole point. We've seen this done where some group members never say a number and others say many. It worked for that group in that moment and it was improvised and not predetermined. If you are facilitating, remember, try not to put any rules onto the group. If they are having difficulty, ask them to relax, take a breath, and try it again—and ask players to try not to try so hard.
3. Try doing this exercise with everyone's eyes closed and then with everyone's eyes open, or in some other inventive way. Some groups have held hands. Create your own version.

Another Exercise to Learn By
Group and Leaderless Mirror

Have the group form a circle with their hands at their sides. In this exercise there is no individual leader. The goal is for the group to somehow find their way to a repetitive movement that the whole group is doing together, without any one player starting, leading, or deciding the movement. To begin, simply ask the group to look around the circle and observe. If they notice something another player is doing (a slight physical motion perhaps), they should unconditionally just begin to follow that motion. The group works very slowly in this way, observing each other's movements. After a short while, players will find the "group mind," at which point they will have found, without discussion, a single, repetitive motion that they are all doing together as a single unit. Once the group has locked into this unified motion, a facilitator may direct them in trying to discover new repetitive motions. Without stopping the motion they are doing, the group, again with no individual leader, slowly begins to transform the motion until they reach a new repetitive motion. Again, this is done by observing and following the group. If the group really gels and finds a group flow, they may move through several different repetitive motions (before they collapse in exhaustion). This exercise reinforces the philosophy of "following the follower" and working as a team, without the direction of an external leader.

Insights

1. In a true statusless group environment, there is no leader. A common phrase in the improv world is "follow the follower," which means at any given moment there is no leader and each individual is following the others in the group, who happen to be following them. If you could draw a picture of "follow the follower," it might look a bit like the infinity symbol ∞. This exercise illustrates this principle wonderfully. If done well, the group will truly find themselves following the followers. It will almost seem magical that the group is moving together because there will truly be no one leading.
2. If there is a facilitator, s/he can help guide the group with some side coaching. The facilitator can ask the group to begin slowly, look around the group, discover something about someone else in the group that is different, and simply follow it. The facilitator can talk the group through finding the flow. This is not necessary but it can be helpful for new groups. The facilitator can also watch for individuals who may be trying to force status or control into the game. While others in the group may not notice it, because they are busy playing the game, an outside observer may be able to catch someone who is trying to change the motion on purpose or who is trying to force the group in a certain direction. There may be others who are reluctant to follow or who "tune out" and really aren't observing with commitment. The facilitator can help the group stay on a statusless track by simply asking those individuals to follow.
3. If you are participating in the exercise, challenge yourself to really let go and follow. There may be times you feel yourself get uncomfortable because the action seems to be going nowhere, or you feel a need to push, or you suddenly have a brilliant idea. Try to stop yourself and simply jump back in to "following." The quickest

way to let go is to return your focus outward to your partners and to simply say yes to them and to the group.
4. If you are a participant and you feel yourself dragging your heels, saying "Oh no, the group is starting to do that motion . . . I don't want to do that . . . no, let's do something else," try to just drop the thought and put your attention back on the group. Simply let go and say yes to what is happening. It will be okay—you're all in it together.

Secret 6

Create a Reward System That Recognizes Innovation & Creative Risk-Taking

We've come to understand that people are generally affected more by their fear of creating the wrong idea than they are motivated by the excitement and passion of creating a truly innovative idea. Time and again I have observed our students, actors, and performers stifle and edit their own ideas because of thoughts like "everyone will think I'm foolish" or "what if it doesn't work." In order to counteract this habit, everyone at the BNW creates and continually practices a system that rewards people for taking risks and sharing their ideas.

We have found that we need to reinforce and reward risk-taking and creative behavior at a 10-to-1 ratio in order to counterbalance human nature's fear of failure. In other words, we praise someone ten times as much for producing a new idea than we critique him/her for a perceived "failure." We also realize that this high level of consistent 10-to-1 affirmation has to be in place for a long time before it will have a positive effect. Most of our students tell us that the most difficult thing to learn about improvisation is that there is no wrong answer or choice. Every day in class we watch students self-edit, bite their tongues, and deny their most instinctual and creative ideas because they believe it is better to say or do nothing rather than to say or do the "wrong" thing.

As you may guess, this learned behavior to self-edit and judge takes a long time to unlearn. Most of our students unlearn it after about six months; however, some take longer and some never change. Even with continuous positive reinforcement, the process can be frustrating and tedious and can require constant effort to overcome.

The simple system we use to reward risk-taking and innovative thinking is to shower an individual with affirmation and positive recognition when they take a risk or blurt out an unedited idea. We have found the affirmations and recognitions that are most effective are oftentimes the simplest, most personal comments or actions; for example, simply saying something like "thank you for the idea" or "I never thought of it that way before" or "I know you're a shy person, so thank you for speaking out" or "that's a really unique perspective." The affirmation does not necessarily have to be formal or public. It nearly goes without saying, but the sincerity with which you recognize these moments is essential. Patronizing language or tone, sarcastic or flippant comments will undermine an individual's ability to believe your affirmations and praise.

Remember that the goal is to improve an individual's skill to mass-produce ideas at the beginning of the idea generation process. By gradually increasing this idea generation, we help an individual to become a more productive part of the theatre and ultimately to improve the overall finished production. Since we know that we need every idea from the outset to produce implementable ideas at the end, we recognize and reward contributions at the start of the creative process with the same level of importance and recognition as we do on opening night.

An Exercise to Learn By
Clams Are Great

The group forms a circle. At all times in this exercise, one person from the group will occupy the center of that circle. The person who is in the center has the task of brainstorming, as fast as possible, the ways that "clams are great" (any object may be chosen in place of clams). They do this by repeatedly completing the sentence, "clams are great because _____." There is no wrong answer and anything can be said to fill in the blank. When any group member in the outer circle feels inspired or feels that the player in the center of the circle is struggling, s/he can jump in, tag out the person in the middle, and continue the game without hesitation. The group works in this manner, always with someone in the middle repeating the phrase and with others randomly jumping in to continue the game as needed, in order to maintain a good flow of ideas.

Players should try to avoid repeating a phrase another member has said. Because you can say anything to complete the phrase, this exercise helps people feel confident and thus supports the rapid acceptance of ideas. It also helps individual members of the group accept their own ideas without judgment, because the group is supporting their creativity and risk taking.

Insights

1. Usually during the first few moments, the most common ideas are generated (i.e., the most logical ideas—"clams are great because they live in the ocean," "clams are great because they are alive," etc.). As the group continues brainstorming, they will discover more creative, random, ridiculous, and brilliant ideas. They don't have to make sense to anyone. Simply committing to an idea and sharing it in the circle is enough. Encourage groups to let whatever idea comes to them be used and embraced.
2. One way to help the player in the middle of the circle is to have the players in the outer circle show their support. When someone is risk-taking in the middle, throwing out their ideas, try having other group members respond to each statement of "clams are great because _____" with some sort of verbal and physical support. It might be as simple as a smile and nodding yes. Better yet, the other players would respond to each statement with a verbal affirmation like "that's right!" or "yes, I know that's true." This immediate positive recognition will instantly boost the confidence of the person in the middle of the circle and will reward him/her for taking the risk to jump in and share. The members in the circle should support each statement with equally positive excitement, whether they have understood the statement or not. This simple adjustment to the exercise demonstrates that recognition and validation for taking risks gives us more confidence to be creative.

3. Remind players that they should be keeping their focus on the person in the middle of the circle, and not thinking ahead to what they might say when they are in the middle. The suggestion in the previous insight (having members in the circle verbally and physically cheer for the person in the middle) will help solve some of this if it is happening. In the same vein, encourage players to jump into the middle even if they don't have an idea, and better yet, *only* if they don't have an idea. Players should jump into the middle when the group and the game need them to jump (i.e., when their teammate is floundering or the flow is slowing), not just when they have an idea.

Another Exercise to Learn By
Press Conference

This exercise proves that when our need to be correct is removed, our creative instincts are empowered. One student is chosen as the "speaker and expert" at a press conference. The other students are "reporters." The speaker is given a topic, preferably one about which s/he knows little; this will be the topic of the press conference. The speaker is instructed that for every question asked, s/he will immediately give an answer as if s/he confidently knows everything about the topic. We are not concerned that the speaker be factually accurate but only that the speaker hears and responds to every question as if s/he knows the answer. The speaker cannot stall by saying "I'm not sure" and cannot negate any question by saying "I don't know the answer." In this way, the speaker learns the skills of self-confidence, of creating on the spot, and of saying yes before s/he has a chance to judge. By removing the need to be correct and accurate, the speaker can only rely on imagination and instinct.

The reporters, in turn, must ask questions as if they know something about the topic, and they must assume that whatever answers the speaker gives are factually accurate. The role of the reporters is not to try to trick or argue with the speaker, but instead to try to really listen to and go along with whatever answers the speaker gives. The reporters' new questions should be inspired by the answers given by the speaker to the reporters' previous questions. In this way, there is a sense of teamwork, listening, and saying yes by everyone in the exercise.

Insights

1. When the ability to fail is taken out of an exercise, we see amazing results. In addition, when we make affirmation and validation a part of the process, players are more creative, more confident, more supportive of others, and more brilliant. When setting up this exercise, we sometimes give the "expert" one simple instruction: No matter what is asked of you, you *know* the answer—simply tell us. We will support you and believe you no matter what you say. Now go. It is then the job of the other group members (and the facilitator, if there is one) to follow through. Treat this person as the expert.

2. Another way to recognize and reward our teammates and partners is to help them go where they are going. This exercise helps us practice that skill. Players who are asking questions should listen carefully to the expert and follow his/her line of thinking when they ask the next question. And vice versa (the expert should hear the questions and answer in a way that honors the question). For example, an expert on asphalt is asked, "I hear you are actually trying to invent a new type of edible asphalt. Tell us about that." The expert can validate his/her partner (the reporter who asked the question) by going in the direction declared; s/he could respond something like, "Yes, I spend weekends in my workshop taste-testing possible alternatives to tar and gravel. I think I've found some candy ingredients that are actually quite promising as pavement alternatives." The next question can also honor the expert, by going along with what s/he has just said, perhaps something like, "Oh, yes, I heard about the possible bubble-gum roads you've been working on. What are some of the positive benefits of such a road?" Sometimes, however, players are unsupportive of their partners, negating their creative ideas. For example, if the expert were asked about edible asphalt and s/he responded, "No, actually it's not edible, it's just more durable." This response not

only negates the reporter's idea (leaving that person feeling pretty bad) but also stops the flow of the game.
3. A common phrase in the improv world is "assume your partner is the best possible partner you could have at that moment." This is a great concept to introduce and practice in this exercise. Everything stated by the expert should be accepted and validated by the group, and every question asked by the group should be accepted and validated by the expert. When this is done, and everyone commits to the spirit of making their partners look good, the creativity, confidence, and brilliance of the members will explode.

Secret 7
Yes, First!

Saying yes to new ideas is by far the most widely understood concept and most basic skill that improvisers use. Building an improvisational scene is a cumulative and reactive exchange. The first improviser declares a point of view or an idea. The second improviser says yes to the idea and then adds to it. This is universally referred to in the improvisation community as the concept of "yes, and" but we refer to it as "yes, first." The opposite of this concept would be "no, but."

As we mentioned earlier, the improvisational scene requires improvisers to figure out who they are, where they are, what needs to get done, and who will do it, and then they must accomplish what they set out to do and resolve the scene in a matter of two to three minutes—all while being funny in front of a live audience. Because of the hyperspeed environment in which improv is produced and performed, saying no to an idea at the beginning of a scene will lead to a temporary shutdown and will require a new set of declarations to restart the action. Improvisers simply don't have the luxury of time to say no.

At the BNW, we believe the true value of saying yes to an idea and then adding to that idea is propulsion, like Jiffy Pop popcorn (see "Idea Generation and the Creative Funnel Process" later in this book). Because our goal is to rapidly produce hundreds of ideas, it is vital and necessary to say yes in order to fill our funnel with ideas. We find that truly innovative solutions are rarely conceived in executable form at infancy. By first saying yes to these ideas, they are propelled through our funnel process toward an innovative end result.

Remember, we are talking about the *first 15 percent* of the idea generation process. We are simply saying yes to the potential that exists within the idea. When we say "yes, first" we are not saying we should immediately put the scene into production or that the idea will be automatically implemented. We are simply saying yes to the idea in order to allow it to reach its full potential. Once we say yes to an idea, it begins to take on the characteristic of fuel for idea generation.

We are aware that saying yes to every idea differs drastically from the norm. Many people in our improv classes initially find it difficult to follow the rules of a simple classroom exercise in which they literally must say the word "yes" before beginning their next sentence of dialogue. But when we are asked, "What is the single most important skill I need in order to become a better improviser?" the answer is, "Say yes, first." And when a students responds, "But what if I disagree with the person's idea?" we commonly reply, "So what?" There is a huge difference between agreeing to implement an idea and simply acknowledging the intrinsic value and potential an idea possesses. Once an individual is practiced in the skill of saying yes, s/he can retain a unique point of view while simultaneously supporting a colleague's points of view, even if the two ideas are at odds with each other.

We encourage everyone in our organization to self-monitor and to maintain a record of the number of times they say "yes, first" as well as "no, but." We challenge you to do the same. If you can increase the number of times you respond to others' ideas with "yes," you are undoubtedly increasing your own and your colleagues' innovative potential.

An Exercise to Learn By

Shared (Two-Person) Story

Two players are selected to share a story with the group. A topic or event is selected—what usually works well is for the two players to retell the events of a common experience they have shared. Once the topic/event is selected, the two players will tell the story together, relaying to the group the details of their shared experience. It should be assumed that both players remember the details of the event, so whatever is declared by one player should immediately be accepted by the other player as what truly happened, and the player who has been listening should add something to the first player's declaration. In this way, the two players are creating the story together, immediately accepting and building off one another's ideas. If the two players share the focus, listen intently, accept all ideas, and build on each other's ideas, the story will come out seamlessly.

Here is an example of how this exercise might develop. Let's assume the topic is "The day we met in high school." The first player jumps in confidently and begins, "I remember the day. She was wearing a pink sweater that was a bit too big. I thought she looked cute." The second player continues, "Yes, my favorite pink sweater. I think I wore it twice a week that year. You were wearing a plaid shirt with holes in the sleeves." Player 1 responds, "That's right. I ripped holes in it that morning in shop class. I was embarrassed about the holes and was trying to role them up while we were waiting in line." Player 2 adds, "Yeah, that's where we first talked . . . waiting in line to get our student ID photos taken." Notice how each person starts by saying yes to the previous statement and then builds directly off the other player's statement.

Insights

1. This exercise sounds very simple, and it can be if players remember one thing: say yes first and then add to whatever you said yes to. Oftentimes, however, players get carried away telling the story or they try to make it a "good" story and they forget the simple way to succeed at this exercise. If there is a facilitator, s/he can help group members stay on task. If they are not saying yes or are not building off their partner's statements, the facilitator can ask the players to slow down and simply say yes first.
2. There are other traps players fall into. Perhaps because s/he is nervous or unconfident, a player might fail to add any information to

the story and simply nod as their partner tells the tale alone. Or a player may act as if s/he really doesn't remember what happened in the story being recounted. If this happens, remind players that they both know exactly what happened and that nothing their partners contribute will be new to them. This will help them avoid questions, which can sometimes get them in trouble (for example, one player might ask, "What happened again after we got our student IDs?"). Usually when a player asks a question during this exercise, s/he is nervous that s/he doesn't have anything to add. Remind this player that what they need to do first and foremost is say yes to their partner's contribution. If they do that and mean it, something will follow. Also, like in so many of these exercises, there is no right or wrong information—no matter what a player says, his/her partner is going to say yes!

3. There are some other subtle tips that can help players in this exercise. One is to have the two storytellers act as if they really like each other and really know each other well. This instant familiarity will help them say yes to one another and will help create rapport. If players are having difficulty saying yes, the facilitator can require them to start every sentence with the word "yes" or a phrase like "that's right," and then require the players to repeat or summarize what their partner said (e.g., "Yes, that's right, I was wearing that pink sweater that was way too big for me . . . and you thought I looked cute"). Once players have done this, they can add something to the story based on what they just repeated.

4. Always saying yes first has another benefit. It forces us to stay in the moment. There is no way to think ahead about what we might say because we cannot say anything until we have heard what our partner has said, which is what we will say yes to. Saying yes first is very liberating if you allow it to be. It frees you from having to think, and thinking is usually a burden to the improviser. It allows you to stay in the moment, to enjoy what your partner is doing, and to jump in and embrace whatever happens next. Saying yes first relieves you of the burden of having to come up with something. There is nothing to come up with. Just say yes first and respond to your partner. It's a very powerful secret. Use it!

Another Exercise to Learn By
Ad Game

In this exercise, the ensemble takes on the role of an advertising team. The goal is for the group to quickly come up with a slogan, a jingle, the packaging, a spokesperson, and other marketing ploys to sell an imaginary product. Usually it helps to have a facilitator. The facilitator will choose an imaginary product for the ad team to work on. The facilitator approaches the group, announcing something like, "Hey gang, we got the 'paper can' account. We've got just a few minutes to come up with an entire campaign to pitch to the 'paper can' people. So let's get to work." The facilitator can then ask questions such as, "Does anyone have an idea for a catchy product name?" Any idea that is thrown out must then be accepted, used, and, above all, praised. If someone says, "How about Port-a-Can?" the facilitator and everyone in the group should immediately respond, "Yeah, great idea!"

The ideas and elements of the marketing campaign that follow should build off the first idea. So, the facilitator might say something like, "Great, the Port-a-Can. What might the packaging look like?" Someone might respond, "It comes with a handle," and someone else adds, "Yes, there's a handle on the box." The facilitator guides the group through the exercise until they have all of the campaign elements. The facilitator or someone in the group may then try to summarize all the elements of the campaign. This exercise is usually a high-energy, fast-paced, positive, and fun game. If the group is truly saying yes first to every idea and is building upon each idea, the campaign will be amusing, creative, and very unique.

Insights

1. This exercise proves that when an idea is immediately met with a yes first, a player gains confidence to contribute more and more ideas. The facilitator should model this and be the first to always say yes. It is inevitable in this exercise that someone will come up with something that either seems odd or is not understood by

the group. The group should still immediately say yes. The group cannot just say yes to ideas that seem "good" or seem like they will work.
2. Saying yes first always takes the group to more creative, more unique, and more unusual places than if they edit and judge ideas along the way. Saying yes first also brings the group to surprising places. It forces them to go in directions they might not have gone had their brains gotten in the way. In this way, saying yes first ensures pure improvisation. It propels players into the unknown without being scary because players trust that others will be saying yes to them. If players only say yes some of the time, this trust will be broken and players will not be able to fully commit to the exercise.
3. As in many of these exercises, some players may get nervous and go into their heads, thinking ahead to what they can add. Or players might try to be funny or shocking, thinking it will help the group. Finally, sometimes the group just gets plain excited and is rattling off so many ideas at once that there is no group cohesion. The facilitator can keep members on track by requiring players to build off the idea before them or s/he can ask the group to slow down and work together.
4. This exercise has produced some pretty innovative and creative marketing campaigns. Every great idea starts somewhere. We believe that all ideas play a role; some may just be building blocks to the greater idea but they are still important building blocks that inspire other ideas. Saying yes first will lead to the next idea, which inspires the next, which in turn inspires the next, and so on. If we listen, say yes first, and build on each other's ideas, we'll arrive someplace surprising and creative.

Secret 8

Perceive Change as Fuel

Improvisers view change quite differently than most people. We often hear that many people are adverse to change and find comfort in stability and consistency. For the improviser, however, if a scene is not changing, then it is stagnant, repetitive, and predictable—and our audience goes away.

It is from this point of view that we approach our perception and appreciation for change. We do not see change as an interruption of what is reliable and consistent but as an exciting exploration toward what is next. Change is not a necessary *evil* but rather a vehicle of *opportunity* that allows us to discover and heighten the next part of the scene.

Our need for change is so strong that we are constantly trying to create new skills that will allow us to promote and ignite change. We are not unhappy with the current situation; instead, we have come to understand that our most innovative ideas come by traveling through a process driven by action and focused on forward movement. The fuel we use to create this forward motion is *change*.

Another contrast we find in our relationship with change, compared to many individuals we encounter, is that we have no need to predict the end result. We don't worry about how impending change might affect us. This freedom from the need to predict the future allows us to focus all of our energy on the current situation. As improvisers, we use the term "being in the moment."

An Exercise to Learn By
One-Word Story

In this exercise, which is done with the group seated in a circle, players will tell an improvised story, one word at a time (i.e., each person adds only one word at a time as the story travels around the circle). In order to create a coherent, meaningful story, the individuals in the group will need to actively listen, release their need to control the outcome of the story, and accept their roles in creating a team product. The group may start with a topic or a word, or may just jump in and begin.

Insights

1. Players must listen carefully so that they hear the story and can contribute appropriately when their turn arrives. Players must also

let go of the need to predict or script the story because no matter how much they try, they cannot inject any control since they are just contributing one word.
2. If players let go of the need to control and instead simply listen and stay in the moment, they will inevitably be surprised by something one of their partners contributes. As hard as players try not to predict the story and influence its direction, there will still be some train of thought going through each person's head as the story evolves. When an unexpected word enters the story, a good improviser sees that as a gift. The unexpected (or "change") is a welcome gift to an improviser. It feels new, exciting, and creative. Because an environment of safety and support has been created, there is no need to fear change; instead, players should embrace the surprise as a brilliant addition to the story.
3. Change and surprise in this exercise serve another purpose—they keep players awake, alert, and ready for action. It's easy to settle in and say, "Oh, I know where this story is going, yes, here we go," and then suddenly someone tosses in a word that is completely out of line with your train of thought. This should be a huge "wake up" and "stay with us" warning. Change keeps players on their toes, and being on your toes is a great place to be as an improviser.
4. Change and surprise in this exercise also force the group to rally together. Something new in the mix, a new direction, a surprising twist, or a creative add-on will offer the group a chance to go somewhere new, which will require teamwork and commitment.
5. If there is a facilitator for the story, that person can watch for group members who might be trying to "force" change into the game. While change is good, forcing something for the sake of control or shock is out of line. The best surprises and change are just that—pure, improvisational, and in the moment.

Another Exercise to Learn By
Newsstand
One person from the group is selected to be a newsstand clerk. This person stands to one side of the group at an imaginary/improvised newsstand. The other group members form a line.

One by one, each member of the line approaches the newsstand with an issue, problem, or need. The newsstand clerk is instructed that s/he is the "world's most helpful newsstand clerk." No matter what the customer asks for, no matter what the problem, the clerk should respond with a positive solution.

For example: Player 1 approaches the newsstand clerk as if someone were chasing him. The clerk begins, "May I help you?" The player says, "Yeah, someone is following me. I need a disguise and I need it quick." The clerk responds, "No problem" while reaching behind an improvised door. "I happen to have an elephant costume here that looks to be your exact size. It's very realistic looking and I've used it to hide from people a number of times. It works brilliantly." Players 1 says, "Oh, this is perfect" and improvises putting the costume on. "I'll just run down the block and hide at the zoo." Once a player has done several rounds as the newsstand clerk, a new player should assume the role of clerk.

Insights

1. The clerk always responds with yes first and then offers whatever solution or product is needed. The player who has approached the clerk should also respond with a yes, by accepting the solution or product offered by the clerk. When players feel they can solve any problem or issue, they are prepared to walk into any unknown situation or deal with any unexpected occurrence in life. They are prepared to be unprepared. Change is not a cause for fear because players know they can improvise and deal with it in the moment.
2. For fun, you might give the players in line suggestions for who they are or attributes they have, as a way to surprise them when they begin. Players who are waiting in line might be thinking of what they can do when it is their turn to speak with the newsstand clerk. Help them refrain from this by tossing out ideas they have to deal with right as their turn is beginning.
3. The clerk must really have an attitude of "whatever is thrown at me next, I can deal with it." Sometimes in this exercise the clerk will balk or freeze or stall. Kindly remind him/her that everything

s/he needs is at his/her fingertips. It's all there, simply jump in and use it. And because his/her partner is going to accept whatever solution s/he offers, success is assured.

4. Sometimes the person receiving the solution balks at or negates the solution given. Using the example given in the exercise description, imagine if the player approaching the newsstand responded, "An elephant costume!? How am I supposed to run in that? Someone is chasing me. Give me something smaller." Help this person recover and instead say yes first. And remind them that they are to use whatever is given to them, even if (and especially if) it is not what they expected.

Part 3
Especially for the Script Writer

Getting Started

We are going to introduce you to a writing process that can be used by anyone, a process that has been proven effective time and again for the BNW actors and writers as well as the Brave New Institute students. This process can serve as a foundation from which you can then develop your own individual process. We hope to take the mystery and fear out of the writing process, so that you can reach a comfort level from which you can access and maximize your best creative energies.

This process is not meant to reduce the amount of creativity and spontaneity that goes into writing. The majority of what ends up on stage should still be born out of an organic process (in improvisation, we refer to this as "the white light"). The greatest asset of any writer will always be raw creativity and the ability to tap into the infinite number of ideas that reside within each of us; however, the best idea in the world cannot be shared, enjoyed, or understood if it is not translated into a form that can be clearly communicated to an audience.

The development of a script takes a fair amount of work and occurs through two processes—the idea generation process and the process of actually crafting the script. Both processes are equally important so you should spend equal time discovering and manufacturing the script. Though it may be a lot more fun to sit around and think about stuff than to pound out a script on a computer, you need to remember that in any occupation, including writing, you are only as good as the products you *create*. Your "job" as a writer is to create and assemble finished scripts. If you are to succeed at that job, you must give as much importance to the utilitarian-execution part of the process as you do to the creative idea-generation process.

Improvisation has always played a huge role in the writing process at the BNW and we believe it can also help you as a writer to generate ideas. Combining the improvisation process and the writing process sometimes may seem awkward, but we feel improvisation can best serve the writing process when:

- It is used in the early part of the writing process, to help generate ideas, premises, and characters.
- It is used as a means of "organic discovery" to help find the initial key elements of a sketch or song. The key elements can include the characters, setting, chain of events, action of the scene, premise, satirical point, and character points of view and reactions as they are put in certain situations.
- It is used to further develop the potential relationship between the key elements that have been discovered.
- It is not relied on to try to force the creation of dialogue (which does not mean that some of the dialogue discovered in an improv may not end up in a final script—in fact, some of the dialogue in the final script often comes from improv, *if* it occurred organically). Trying to improvise a scene in order to "find dialogue" is nearly impossible; once you've stated that your purpose is to "get dialogue," you've eliminated the possibility of an organic scene. In an improv scene, you're *discovering*; in the scripting process, you're *manufacturing* something based on the key elements you discovered in the improv process. It's nearly impossible to find dialogue in and of itself without first having this discovery process.

Our improvisational goal in the writing process is to produce ideas, not dialogue. You shouldn't try to think of ideas but instead try to adhere to the BNW improvisational philosophies and let the ideas show themselves through the improvisational process. For example, you could improvise a montage or a series of scenes inspired by the theme or suggestion of gun control. After improvising fifteen to twenty organic scenes, you hopefully will have seen many different characters, points of view, locations, and situations. At this point, you can identify the key elements (characters, premises, points of view, settings, and situations) of the montage that you like. You can then improvise scenes that combine and further explore some of these key elements. For example, "Let's do a scene in which the 'NRA guy who's afraid of guns' and the 'gun-toting elderly nun' are both at a political rally, during which a sniper shows up—and let's see what happens." Embracing this premise of the role of improvisation in the writing process, you can use improv to create what we refer to as the key elements of the sketch or script.

Using this process for idea generation, you may sometimes just find the characters for your script and at other times you may find everything except the location. We recommend you always use improvisation as a way to find the key elements of a sketch first, before diving into "scripting" the sketch. Our philosophy is that the best way to find unique and truthful elements or ideas for a sketch is through honest scenic improvisation, and the best way to write dialogue for a sketch is to "fill in the blanks" based on the key elements that you have created or discovered through improvisation. The key elements should give you all that you need to manufacture the dialogue.

The Sketch-Writing Process

There are many times within the rehearsal process that we discover or stumble upon simple premises, bits, visual gags, sound bits, blackouts, or technical elements that are funny and add to the overall quality of a review show. These elements are often the benefits and products of the execution of the writing process we've just described. Below, we outline the steps to take to help find the key elements for your sketch.

Step 1: Find the Jumping-off Point

The jumping-off point (sometimes also called the "moment of inspiration") can be anything—a satirical point, a character, an idea, a situation, a word, a theme. For example, "I want to explore a sketch about President Clinton's relationship to interns" or "I have this idea about a woman who wants to be a loon." This jumping-off point can come about in a number of ways:

1) You can develop it through an improvisation process.
2) A specific event that happens in the world can trigger it.
3) Something might happen in your own life to trigger it.
4) It might simply pop into your head without you really knowing why.

We have observed that the best way to produce these inspirational moments is to have a very active and diverse life. Get outside the theatre, read the newspaper, have a wide variety of friends, maximize your life experiences. This is the research component of your job as an actor/writer.

Step 2: Find and Create the Key Elements of the Sketch

In this step, you create and brainstorm all the key elements for the sketch. This is one of the steps for which the BNW utilizes improvisation. We believe it is important to find all of these elements before you begin scripting, but the order in which you find them and the process by which you find them will differ almost every time. Here is a list of the key elements:

1) **The Satirical Point**

   What is the message of the sketch or song? What do you want the audience to know about your opinion on the topic of the sketch? An example: "Allowing citizens to carry automatic weapons is ridiculous."

2) **The Characters**

   The most important part of the character development is point of view. Points of view are attitudes, beliefs, and opinions the character holds—more specifically, the attitudes, beliefs, and opinions the character holds with regard to the satirical point of the sketch. Sometimes we find factual elements of the character description that help us discover the character's point of view. Factual elements can include occupation, age, ethnic background, marital status/sexual orientation, geographic origin, etc. Another important aspect of character is what Michael Shurtleff calls the "fighting for": What is this person "about" in this scene? What is this person's goal in this scene? What is this person trying to accomplish and what is s/he fighting for? What is this person's "bottom line"? It is very important that both the writer and the audience be able to easily define the character's point of view.

3) The Action of the Scene

This can also be called the plot, the path, the conflict, etc. It might also be called "the beginning, the middle, and the end" of the scene. Remember that your choice of action will create a rhythm, and always be aware of how that rhythm affects the clarity and humor of the scene. It is very important to find the resolution or ending of a scene. Sketches that don't have endings seem vague to most audiences.

4) The Environment, Location, or Setting

Because we are a minimalist theatre (i.e., not many props, costumes, or sets), it is vital that the BNW clearly communicates to the audience where the scene takes place. Regardless of how elaborate your staging is, the setting affects the points of view of the characters and the action of the scene. For example, two guys discussing politics in a diner would play much differently than two guys from death row discussing politics in electric chairs. Don't forget that environment also includes mood, tone, temperature, color, and time (both time of the day and of the year).

5) A Personal Explanation of Why You Think the Scene Is Funny (or Sad or Insightful)

In your explanation, try to explain why you and the audience will think this sketch, these characters, and the action of this scene are funny. Is it a sight gag or a physical gag? Is the premise funny? Have we explored a topic through an unusual angle?

Step 3: Organize Your Key Elements

In this step, you document and organize your key elements. This organization can take many forms: a sketch outline, completing a sketch worksheet (see appendix 1 at the back of the book as well as the attached CD-ROM), writing a "beat sheet," or any form that enables you to (1) get all of the key elements down on paper and (2) get a view of the whole sketch from start to finish (this step is not complete unless you know what the major beats of the scene are from start to finish).

We encourage you to improvise your scene after you have completed this step, incorporating the key elements of the sketch as suggestions for the scene. What seems to be difficult at this point is that the "obligation" to include all the key elements in your improvised version of the sketch may feel restrictive and predictable.

Step 4: Fill in the Blanks between the Key Elements with Dialogue

This is the step where you actually sit at the computer and type the script. At the end of this step you should have your first draft of a finished script. Remember, if you truly have identified all the key elements, the dialogue should produce itself and simply reinforce the characters, the satirical point, and the action of the scene. If this step seems difficult, it is possible that steps 2 and 3 are incomplete.

Step 5: Perform the Script with Your Fellow Cast Members and Your Director

We often get tunnel vision when writing. The energy that is created by taking a script to its feet at performance level will reveal many things. We need to perform the sketch and learn from the act of performing and from the reactions and observations made by our fellow cast members and directors.

Here is a list of questions to ask when observing or evaluating a sketch:

1) Does the sketch reinforce all the key elements?
2) Does the sketch communicate a clear and definable idea?

Especially for the Script Writer

3) Do the characters have clear points of view?
4) Is the action and dialogue true to the points of view of the characters?
5) Is the environment well defined?
6) Does the environment support or detract from the satirical point of the sketch?
7) Are there any jokes that can be easily written and inserted into the scene that reinforce the satirical point?
8) Did the scene make you laugh?
9) Does the sketch seem to have a point of focus by the characters? Do we understand who the characters are—i.e., their roles (ambiance, antagonist, etc.)?
10) If a scene has a "game" in it, is it clearly defined and is it being well played?
11) Is there enough exposition, especially at the beginning of the scene, to allow the audience to understand what is going on?
12) Is the scene attractive to the eyes and ears?
13) Do you feel the sketch can be defined as "brave and new," or does it seem "cheap and old"?

Step 6: Do the First Rewrite

Make specific script changes based on what you learned by performing the sketch and from the observations you received from your fellow cast members and your director.

Step 7: Perform the Sketch in Front of an Audience Other Than Your Fellow Cast Members and Your Director

You will learn different things from this performance, including:

1) Do people outside your process understand the main point and the key elements of the scene?
2) Are there things you thought were funny, which in fact were not funny; and vice versa (i.e., unexpected things got a laugh)?
3) Is the sketch accessible to the audience, or does it isolate them?
4) What was the general reaction by the audience, the general feeling the sketch created for them?

Step 8: Do a Second Rewrite

Rewrite the sketch based on the audience's reaction and the comments from your fellow cast members and your director.

Step 9: Continue to Perform the Sketch

Continue to perform the sketch, always remaining aware of what you are learning with each performance and always making adjustments as needed. This step continues through the run of the show and through the life of the sketch.

Often the simple act of going through this nine-step process can create new directions, new ideas, and new key elements (in the middle of the process). As a rule of thumb, trust your gut; if the new direction and new key elements feel better, don't be afraid to change the direction of the sketch midstream. However, know that the goal is a finished script and that it is better to rework and edit a finished script than to endlessly rework an unfinished script or concept.

Also remember that this process will be different for each sketch you develop. Some sketches are perfect on first writing and some sketches need five rewrites. Be warned that going through many rewrites can result in overworking a sketch. If this is happening, go back to the original, organic point or analyze whether one or some of the key elements are not well defined, resulting in a "difficult" sketch.

Collecting Comedic Tools

There are many "tools" you will collect as you become a more experienced writer. These are premises and structures that can be used over and over to create quality sketches. Don't feel that it is unoriginal to use some of these tools as you are constructing your sketches and as you are following this process. There is a reason why these tools work, so it is good to understand them. As long as your specific premise, concept, and idea are original, organic, and truthful, you should view these tools as ways to increase your productivity and your efficiency as a sketch writer. A tiny list of examples of these tools includes:

1) Reusable Environments—like a game show, news broadcast, or concert.

2) Parodies—a parody of a commonly known show, song, relationship, character, etc.
3) Reusable Characters—recycling a stereotypical character to add comic relief (i.e., the "bumbling idiot sidekick").
4) Reusable Bits—commonly used tricks or gimmicks (i.e., mistaken identity, mimicking someone, prat falls, spit takes, etc.).

Part 4
Practical Applications

Idea Generation and the Creative Funnel Process

The Brave New Workshop uses the funnel process to create our mainstage shows, as well as just about every project throughout the company—regardless of length—from a five-minute brainstorming session to a three-year implementation of a strategic plan. You can use this process to "finalize" your script, to work out the kinks in your show, or to create and implement a new strategic plan for your theatre. This process incorporates the eight secrets we discussed earlier in the book into an "editing" process of sorts that leads to an innovative and fresh artistic end result.

The example we use to illustrate the funnel process is the development of a one-hour-and-forty-five-minute script to be performed on our main stage in Minneapolis. In a matter of fifty-six days of work, eight cast members begin with one word of inspiration and then execute the funnel process that ultimately leads to our opening night performance.

Like any theatre company, we work hard to ensure that the quality of our shows is consistent and reliable. We also experience the typical challenges of maintaining that quality over time, challenges like the talent and experience of our actors and writers; the political and economic climates that exist in our state and the country at large during the time of our production; and even which popular icons are in or out of fashion. Because we have many variables, and a long history of quality to live up to, we realize the only real assurance we have in the end result of our work is that we strictly adhere to our idea generation process. Diligently executing the steps in the funnel process has proven to be much more reliable than stumbling on a brilliant idea, a talented actor, or the ideal market conditions. Our funnel process goes like this:

Step 1—Idea Generation

The focus of our first step is volume. We understand that initially it is the quantity of ideas that is most important, rather than the quality or the ability to implement them. We consider ourselves mass producers at this point and pay no attention to the perceived value of an idea. We simply need to produce as many ideas as we can, as fast as we can. This mass production of ideas reinforces our belief that great ideas are rarely ever created in an implementable form. Several dozen or perhaps hundreds of ideas must be created in order to produce a single viable and profitable idea.

For our production, which typically requires twenty-five sketches or songs to make up an opening night script, we find we need to produce 600 one-sentence ideas. To achieve this volume of ideas, it is important to adhere to the eight secrets discussed earlier in this book. The secret most essential for this specific step of idea generation is the secret of deferring judgment.

For us to create 600 one-sentence ideas, it typically takes three eight-hour stream-of-consciousness brainstorming sessions. We refer to these 600 ideas as the Master Inspiration List. The Master Inspiration List is used throughout the entire fifty-six-day funnel process and each team member uses it as a reference point. It also serves as a way for team members to recall the energy and excitement of the first three days of rehearsal, to help keep ideas fresh throughout the process.

Our process begins with the introduction of a word or phrase to be used as inspiration for the overall theme of the show. This word or phrase is simply a jumping-off point, representing a concise definition of a theme of topical interest to our audience. This theme is often an inspiration for the title of the show as well. As you can see from the following list of titles and corresponding themes, our titles are often a barometer of what is happening in America at the time the show is in production:

- "I'm Okay, You're a Jerk" (1981; self help)
- "I Compute, Therefore IBM" (1983; the computerization of America)
- "Yuppie See, Yuppie Do" (1985; excessiveness)
- "The Viceman Cometh" (1986; addiction)
- "Victim Nation: The Don't Blame Me Revue" (1994; responsibility)
- "Cinderella and the Glass Ceiling" (1994; women in the workplace)
- "Saving Clinton's Privates, or Swallow the Leader" (1998; need we say?)
- "Prozac: It's What's for Dinner, or Let the Side Effects Begin" (2000; the answer is to medicate)
- "Martha Stewart, Prison Vixen" (2003; entitlement)

Once a theme is announced, idea generation begins. We compare idea generation to Jiffy Pop popcorn because of the speed and exponential quality of our productivity. It looks like a group of people casually sitting in a comfortable environment with two people typing as fast as they can in order to make sure all the ideas are recorded.

Step 2—Refinement

The secret most essential to step 2 of this funnel process is the secret of sharing focus and accepting all styles. During this phase, each individual approaches the key elements in his/her unique way and communicates to the group in his/her unique style. We support the sharing of focus and the acceptance of all styles as a way to ensure that each cast member can create and communicate ideas in a way most comfortable for him/her.

Each cast member is asked to take responsibility for twenty to twenty-five ideas and to place their initials next to these ideas on the Master Inspiration List. They are encouraged to choose ideas they are most passionate about further exploring or ideas that elicit outrage within them. In other words, the ones that get them most fired-up.

Once assigned, cast members immediately begin work on the next part of the process, the key elements. The purpose of the key elements is to create a format so that the essential ingredients of the show can be recorded, organized, and understood. Over the years, we have found that the simple step of idea organization can be a huge stumbling block. Our writers would simply let an idea slip away into oblivion if they were not able to succinctly communicate the components that make up that idea. By creating a simple worksheet and format for our cast members to follow and complete, we discovered the right blend of innovation and organization.

We ask cast members to identify and thoroughly define the most essential building blocks of the product—in our case, a comedy sketch. For our purposes, those building blocks are (1) the satirical point, (2) a description of the characters, (3) the action points of the scene, (4) a thorough description of the environment in which the scene will take place, and (5) a personal explanation of why they believe the idea is funny.

In our process, individuals are not necessarily required to compile all five aspects of the key elements in a sketch worksheet. It is often acceptable and encouraged for each cast member to present a partially completed key-element worksheet to the group, which relieves pressure from that idea's author and allows everyone to begin a collaborative and multifaceted approach to each idea. Deferring judgment still plays an important role at this stage in the process, as we are in the infancy of that idea's development.

Step 3—Collaboration

As individual team members work to complete the sketch worksheets for the ideas they have chosen, our process enters its next phase. The secret that is most essential to step 3 of the funnel process is the secret of "yes, first!" We are now in the mode of idea explosion and need to take the idea we are working on in its most raw and simple form, saying yes to its potential, its growth, and to the rest of the group.

We have learned that the simple practice of saying the words "yes, and" allows us to take a one-sentence version of an idea and inflate it into a thoroughly fleshed-out key element or idea. When we are practicing the secret of "yes, first!" in this step, the process is akin to those capsules you put in your tub, add water to, and thirty seconds later they are a two-foot-in-diameter sponge dinosaur. I'm sure that's exactly what it will seem like to you.

This phase of collaboration typically lasts for two weeks. Cast members present complete or incomplete sketch worksheets, one idea at a time. They can present them orally and/or distribute a hard copy to the group. Once the worksheet is presented to the group, a discussion takes place that involves both critique and new idea generation.

One critical tool we have developed, which we use with diligence and discipline, is a very specific vocabulary to discuss and critique each other's key elements. We have developed an actual glossary of terms that specifically refer to the person's *work*, not to the individual person. By using language that clearly separates the work from the individual, we have been able to achieve an environment in which a group can improve a set of key elements and offer new ideas without apprehension or worry about hurting a colleague's feelings. For example, in discussing a work, some questions we might ask include:

- Is the pace of the scene adequate?
- Have we adequately heightened the action of the scene?
- Is the satirical point redundant?
- Is there enough exposition in the first thirty seconds of the scene for the audience to understand the who, what, where, why, and how?
- Are the characters based in a minimal amount of reality, as a means to make them at least identifiable to the audience, if not likeable?
- Is there a way to say the same thing in one sentence instead of five sentences?
- What percentage of our audience will or will not understand the reference being made within the sketch (i.e., references should not be too obscure)?
- Is there a way to get to the action of the scene faster?
- Are we showing as much as we are telling?

The point of all this is to ensure that we are observing and then helping the sketch without critiquing and then hurting the writer. By the very nature of our work, and sometimes by the nature of our personalities, writers and performers can react *personally* to critiques of their work. We encourage all our writers and performers to continually develop a thicker skin when it comes to observations aimed at improving their work.

Along with a specific critical vocabulary, other tools that we use to improve and complete the key elements for a sketch are:

1. Ideas are improvised on stage by the entire cast. The beta version of this concept is executed in several different ways by the improvisers. This working-on-our-feet process allows us to look at the idea differently or to find a specific aspect of the key elements that was not apparent through typical group discussion.
2. Oftentimes we will examine whether or not the specific key element we are trying to complete would perhaps be better served if it was incorporated or combined with another Master Inspiration List idea or key element currently being explored.

We are very conscious at this point in the process that certain ideas can organically lose their ability to make us passionate about them. Because we are still in the widest point of the funnel and are still concerned with quantity and not quality, we embrace the option that perhaps it is simply better to move on to the next idea and eliminate this one or put it on the proverbial back-burner. Because we always maintain a copy of the Master Inspiration List and any key elements that have been started, we often find ourselves later in the process discovering a different use for an idea.

Once the entire group has had the opportunity to provide input to the key elements of an idea and the sketch worksheet has been completed, the group (ultimately the director) decides whether the idea is ready for the next step or if it needs to be set aside for now. This is the first point in our creative process at which the director begins to act as editor, taking responsibility for deciding which ideas will continue through the funnel process. It also qualifies ideas to enter the next step, the creation of the first draft script.

Step 4—Engineering

The secret most essential to this step is to create a statusless environment. We need to ensure that both the author of the individual script and the cast members who critique it feel creatively safe. In order for the cast to truly achieve a level of dialogue that is without reservation or bias, everyone in the group must feel comfortable and safe to speak freely and to communicate bluntly. Because we drastically reduce the amount of classic office-drama, we increase the speed at which we refine our product.

The individuals who are accountable for the ideas they chose from the Master Inspiration List will now begin to transform the key elements into a first draft of a script. These script drafts are presented to the group and read aloud. Oftentimes we read them on stage and on our feet as a way to involve our bodies and to ensure the pacing and energy needed in reading the script is present.

After the script is "performed" for the first time, the group members discuss how they feel about the script, making sure they use specific vocabulary separating the work from the person who wrote it. Since the individuals in the group are discussing, making observations, and sometimes critiquing another cast member's work, we are very conscious of maintaining an environment that does not create negative stimuli for either the author or the critics. You will hear terms such as "pace" or "intensity," "the need for resolution," "heightening," "redundancy," "the need for specificity," and similar terms that are emotionless and clearly attached to the document and not to the author.

After group members make their observations and facilitate discussion, the director decides what changes or additions need to be made to that version of the script. The script-change recommendations are the author's homework and are usually done outside the rehearsal process. This read-discuss-revise process lasts all the way until opening night; many sketches are rewritten more than five times before they reach their final form. This is the first point in the process at which we begin to evaluate whether or not the sketch becomes part of our final production. Typically we write first drafts for approximately sixty key elements and only about twenty-five make it to the stage as a completed sketch and as part of the final production.

As the scripts become more and more refined, the director begins to change his/her view from seeing them as individual pieces to considering the relationship they might have with each other. S/he examines how they may be organized in a way that will create a successful show. At the end of this phase, the director may have even gone so far as to create his/her first draft of a "running order" or show outline.

Another common practice at this stage in our creative process is that we purposely transfer the ownership and responsibility of the idea to another cast member. We do this in order to get a new perspective and approach.

Step 5—Focus Groups

The secret that is most essential to this step is sharing focus and accepting all styles. We now begin to share focus with our new cast member, the audience. We focus our eyes and ears toward our customers. We watch and listen not only for their laughter or applause, but keenly observe their attention span, their body language, and their fidgetiness. We listen without egos. There is an endless list of theatres that no longer exist because it was clear to them their audience was "wrong."

One of the wonderful luxuries of the live-theatre business is we have a focus group consisting of actual customers every time we perform a show. We are able to extract customer-satisfaction information and test our next production in real time with real customers.

We maximize this nightly focus group by performing the scripts we are working on for show "B" for the audience that just watched show "A." After show "A" takes its bow, the director takes the stage and tells the audience that tonight they will have the opportunity to see some "works in progress" from the new show we are writing. The director informs the audience that the actors will have scripts in hand and will not be accompanied by the props and costumes that may eventually be used in the scene. Because our theatre is in Minnesota and is often filled with very passive and stoically nice individuals, we have to aggressively prompt the audience to give honest and audible reactions. We let them know they are part of our process and we appreciate their input as a way to provide them with the best possible comedy we can produce.

While the script is performed, the director and cast members who are not performing watch the action on stage and gauge the audience's reaction. They gather volumes of information from the audience regarding the content, pace, delivery, and tone of the show being tested. The audience responses are noted in detail and are used to refine the script and determine whether (1) it needs to be shorter, (2) it needs to end differently, (3) a character needs to be removed, (4) the material is appropriate for an entire sketch, and/or (5) two sketches should be combined into one.

This is the first part of our process, during which market constraints begin to show themselves. For every show, there are sketches for which our audiences do not necessarily share the cast's opinion of the quality of the product. In these cases, the scripts sometimes need to be drastically changed or even eliminated. Because we produce so many ideas at the beginning of our funnel process, we do not have to go back to the drawing board; we simply have to refocus our energies, for example, on script 42 instead of script 36.

Step 6—Road Testing

The secret that is most essential to this step is perceiving change as fuel. Just when we think we are close to completion and believe things will become more consistent and predictable, preview week begins. There is no doubt that the immense changes that happen within this short period of the funnel process drastically increase our workload. We welcome these changes because we realize the magnitude of their importance in producing a show that meets our audiences' expectations. Oftentimes these changes also provide insight for our actors that would not have happened if we had simply settled for a show that was easy to perform or that was "generally acceptable" to our audience. The expectation we have set with our audiences over the last forty-five years is that each new show will be better than the last. We need to live up to our reputation for cutting-edge satirical comedy theatre.

We are now eight days from opening night. The actors lovingly refer to this period of time as "hell week." We have created opening and closing numbers. We have incorporated transitions between our sketches and songs. We have reset the lights in our theatre, designed and constructed costumes and props, memorized our lines, and learned our choreography and blocking. Now it's time to see if the ship floats.

Typically the director now narrows the scripts to approximately two hours' worth of material, of which fifteen to twenty minutes will be cut over the next seven days. The director also creates a running order of scripts, which is likely to be altered after each of the five preview-week performances.

Preview week is the first time our audiences are exposed to our new show in its fully rehearsed and polished form. This step in the funnel is challenging because we have a short period of time during which to change many things: we are always performing one show while writing another; there is often crossover within the cast (some members of the current show are also in the new show); and we typically open the new show one weekend after we close the current show. Our average show-run varies from twelve to sixteen weeks. We have created a situation that many theatres would find unreasonable and perhaps impossible. Although this self-created obstacle presents swift challenges, it is one of the most important characteristics of our work and it differentiates us from our competition. It also creates a sense of urgency that we believe drives our creativity.

This part of the process is difficult for the cast members. They are tired and have a tendency to begin to doubt the quality of the show. Like all of us at times, they would rather be "done" than rework the show yet again. Each night after preview performances, we make drastic changes in the sketch line-up and the casting, and we are still determining which scripts to include. Each day, we rehearse a new version of the show, from start to finish, and then perform the new version for the next night's audience. After the final preview performance and more than fifty days of hard work, we have finally refined our show in a way that is most attractive to our audience. We are ready for opening night.

Step 7—Product to Market

The secret that is most essential to this step is declarations. Our team is responsible for creating the production *and* delivering it to our audience; therefore, we need to promote the team's confidence skills, stage presence, and declarative behavior. There is a drastic difference in simply "presenting it" to the audience and "performing it" before the audience. Without being arrogant, we need to have our cast hit the stage and deliver the material in a way that says "We are excited and proud of our show, and you should be too." This declarative style of delivery is sometimes referred to as salesmanship.

Six hundred ideas, one hundred key elements, sixty first-drafts of scripts, fifty-six days of rehearsal, eight cast members, five nights of previews, and it all comes down to one night, opening night. To put our show in perspective, the actual amount of material we perform on opening night is equal to five episodes of a prime-time sitcom. Oh, and by the way, it's live—we only have one shot.

Like any small theatre producing its own show, opening night raises anxieties and questions like "Will the audience like it?" or perhaps more importantly "Will they like it enough to pay for it?" As one of the few completely self-sustaining theatres in the country, we are intimately aware of the relationship between ticket sales and profitability. During some years, it has been the relationship between ticket sales and existence.

On opening night, there are typically four to six theatre critics in the audience. The difference between positive or negative reviews has the potential to affect ticket sales and revenues by 40 to 50 percent over a twelve-week run of the show.

As we arrive at the bottom of our funnel process on opening night, there is a drastic increase in the tension and energy of our cast, compared to the first day of rehearsal. There is tremendous pressure on our cast to perform at a level that meets the standards of our theatre and lives up to our reputation. We are also very cognizant that we need to generate next week's ticket sales.

So where does the confidence in our production come from? Is it in the individual talents of the cast members? Perhaps. Is it the trust the cast has in the director? Maybe. Mostly, however, this confidence is found in the well-proven and consistent outcome that our creative funnel process ensures.

Remember, our shows typically run for a twelve- to sixteen-week period. We encourage the cast to continually discover new ways to improve the show during its lifespan. We use a specific process of nightly evaluation to discover new and innovative ways to improve the show. We have found that a team member's level of commitment to improve the show is directly related to the amount of ownership they have in the actual creation of that production.

Summary

I would like to say that our creative process was born out of insight and brilliance, but the truth is, it is a result of necessity and survival. Like many theatres, we have unique challenges that are specific to our productions. For example:

1. Every show is an original piece of work created by our team;
2. We are always creating one show while we are performing another;
3. We have a limited market-testing period; and
4. There is a tremendous amount of pressure to create a production that lives up to our forty-five year reputation for innovative, cutting-edge comedy.

In order to create an innovative product within the above parameters, we have had to develop consistency in a process filled with variables. The process is so important and has proven so effective that it is revered and respected by our company members and it is rarely challenged. When outsiders ask, "How have you been able to create fresh and marketable shows throughout the conservative '50s, the turbulent '60s, the psychedelic '70s, the excessive '80s, the apathetic '90s, and the unpredictable new millennium?" we reply, "We follow the funnel."

Perhaps at this point you're saying, "Wow, sounds like a cool process, good for you, but unfortunately, I don't work in a theatre that produces comedy scripts, I work in a theatre that produces works of dramatic intensity, or historical pieces, or. . . ." We've shared our funnel process with a wide variety of individuals, schools, and theatre artists, many not in the comedy business. They have all been able to successfully adapt our process and to implement it within their own cultures. The results I have witnessed have been remarkable. I am thoroughly convinced our process is applicable to any group of people who want to find the next great idea.

The Miracle of Imperfection

Remember that part of improvisation is accepting the imperfection of the art form. This is a reality for us every day. Our creative process has shown us that most "mistakes" lead to the next unexpected innovation, the next great script, the next brilliant scene. We never find value in dwelling on what we did not accomplish. We are most interested in what we can, and will, accomplish. We have been able to continually produce a show our audiences love, and we have gained a reputation for being innovative and irreverent and constant. We have accomplished this year after year because we cling to the secrets we've just shared with you.

We believe that by employing our eight secrets along with our creative funnel process, you can accomplish your goal of becoming a comedy sketch writer; or your goal as a playwright of improving your organizational skills; or your goal as a performer of increasing your spontaneity; or your goal as a director of renewing your insight and your creative prowess; or even your goal as an administrator of finding new venues to keep your theatre alive. Keep laughing, and the next time you visit the Twin Cities, come take in a show at the Brave New Workshop or participate in one of our classes. We'd love to meet you and to hear how our process has helped you to realize your goals!

The BNW Rehearsal Process

The following narrative describes the process by which mainstage shows are developed at the Brave New Workshop. While this process varies from director to director and from cast to cast, it is meant to serve as a guide in the creative flow of the show development and the rehearsal period.

Pre-rehearsal Prep Work

Show Content and Format Is Chosen

You will need to decide what the intent, focus, and format of your show will be. The Brave New Workshop Comedy Theatre mainstage productions are always:

- Comedy.
- Satirical.
- In revue format.
- Improvisation-based.

A Theme Is Developed

Most BNW revues have some relation to a theme that serves as a through-line to link the sketches and songs. The theme is usually not very specific; for example, "sex" or "fashion" or "censorship." This theme is used as a template, giving an overall logic or focus point to the fifteen to twenty-five pieces in the show. The use of a theme is not a necessity—the show can simply be a compilation of unrelated satirical sketches and musical pieces—but themes have served our productions well because they give our revue format theatrical touchpoints and form. The theme should be decided upon well in advance of the start of the rehearsal period.

The Show Is Given a Title

The title of the show sometimes reflects the theme and is created through our funnel process. It is one of the most important aspects of the process because it is the single biggest reason guests decide to come to the show. Because we produce original material, our ability to test the material of the show before the run is limited. The show's title has to make a person laugh and draw them to the show.

A Pre-rehearsal Cast Meeting Is Held

The pre-rehearsal cast meeting takes place one week (or more) prior to the start of rehearsals and has the following goals:

- Introduce new cast members.
- Introduce the director.

- Discuss the theme of the show.
- Discuss the rehearsal and writing process.
- Assignment(s) for the first day of rehearsal are given.

The Rehearsal Period

Currently the average BNW rehearsal and writing period is six weeks. While this timing can vary, six weeks seems to be an adequate amount of time for the BNW to create a show, starting from the first day of rehearsal through to the first preview performance.

Week One
- The "pot" is filled with sketch ideas, concepts, and points of view. We call this our Master Inspiration List.
- The theme is discussed and is dissected into subtopics.
- The director leads a discussion of the potential "feel" and "tone" of this particular show.
- Daily warm-ups are done.
- The musical director begins developing musical styles and themes, and s/he leads group vocal exercises.
- The technical director begins to generate design concepts based on themes and subtopics (the design includes the set, video, recorded music, and lighting).

Often the beginning of each day is group-discussion time, which can concern a topic as broad as a news article or an individual point of view on a subtopic, or a topic as narrow as a specific sketch or song idea. It is critical to stress that the BNW cast is a writing team; the responsibilities for research, scripting, and idea generation lie with the entire cast. The director serves as an editor-in-chief throughout the writing and rehearsal period.

During this first week, writing outside of rehearsal is encouraged, with each cast member given assignments for further research or scripting. Daily vocal and physical warm-ups are a must; vocalization exercises include musical work on harmonies and blending. The "group mind" is developed through daily improvisation.

Week Two
- Daily warm-ups and assignments continue.
- The sketch list has been expanded.
- Specific ideas are in key-elements form.
- Musical-theme development continues; song lyrics begin to be written and improvised.
- Vocalization, blending, and harmony work continues.
- A couple of sketches/ideas hit the stage in rehearsal.
- Ideas are improvised on stage in rehearsal.

Week Three
- Daily warm-ups and assignments continue.
- More sketches/ideas hit the stage in rehearsal.
- Sketches that have been advanced to the draft stage are presented in brief read-through and forum discussion. Edits are proposed.
- Completed sketches begin to be put "in the bank."
- Music lyrics on existing song ideas continue to be explored and written.
- Improvisations are show and sketch specific.
- Possible links between pieces are discussed.
- The costumer has the first consultation on show clothes and special costume pieces.
- Specifics of some video, audio, and prop needs are listed and worked through.

Week Four
- Daily warm-ups and assignments continue.
- More sketches/ideas hit the stage in rehearsal and some are performed during the improvisation set that takes place after the currently running show.
- Show-specific, sketch-specific improvisation now occurs.
- The show's opening and closing should begin to be discussed and improvised.
- More first-draft sketches and some second-draft sketches are developed.

- More first-draft and some second-draft music lyrics are prepared.
- Reviews and edits continue to be made.
- Finished sketches are "in the bank."
- Second version of master sketch list is prepared.
- Possible links between pieces are further discussed.
- Technical considerations heat up. The technical director begins to schedule blocks of time to view the work-in-progress.

We're at the halfway point now, deep into scripting first drafts and even some second drafts. New topics are discussed at the beginning of each day. It's necessary to continue to improvise close to half of the time, whether it's a brief pass at a sketch idea brought up early in the day or a sketch-specific improvised development. The pace of writing and presenting finished drafts quickens. More assignments stem from discussions.

Week Five

- Daily warm-ups and assignments continue.
- Sketches are in first, second, and even third drafts by the beginning of this week.
- Every high-contention sketch should have hit the stage in rehearsal at least once by now.
- Sketches with promise are given rewrite direction.
- The show's opening and closing are drafted in more detail.
- More sketches/ideas hit the stage in set after the currently running show.
- Possible links between pieces continue to be discussed, with some firm links established.
- The third version of the master sketch list is prepared.
- A "fun-through" occurs this week. The show, in its raw form, is performed for the rest of the staff of the company.
- Show clothes are purchased and more costume pieces are discussed and designed or purchased.
- The technician has scripts and technical notes on all existing pieces. Video and audio pieces are scheduled or are on their way toward completion.

New topics are discussed at the beginning of each day. By week five, there probably will be fifty to sixty active, written, or partially written, pieces. Some pieces are dropped completely at this point.

Week Six (Tech Week/Hell Week)
- Daily warm-ups and assignments continue.
- Transitions and blackouts are given some stage time.
- Most scripts and songs are into third or fourth or final drafts.
- The director shifts focus to more performance notes.
- Show line-up is discussed.
- The show's opening and closing are fully written and developed.
- More sketches/ideas hit the stage in set in the currently running show.
- The technician has full working knowledge of all pieces. Cues are written.
- All known props are purchased.
- Specialty costume pieces are completed and delivered.
- A first draft of the show line-up is completed.
- The sketch list is pared down to show length (plus 15 to 20 percent).
- Pieces are reedited.
- New transitions are solidified.
- Run-throughs are scheduled.
- Show line-up is adjusted after each run-through, if necessary (it always is).
- All technical elements are in place. The technical director concentrates on running the show and on refinement of cues.
- All props and costumes are delivered and are available for use during rehearsals.
- A minimum of four full tech run-throughs should be performed before the first preview (Sunday, Monday, Tuesday, and Wednesday prior to the first preview).

Hell week begins! We typically run individual pieces during the day and perform the run-throughs in the early evening. The challenge now is to reach show readiness for all individual sketch and musical pieces. Rewrites come quickly, with a minimum of discussion. The director's challenge is to pace the week to keep the cast's energy focused at a consistent level. The technical director's challenge is to complete all major projects relating to the show early, so s/he can fully concentrate on running sketches in rehearsal.

Preview Week
- Line-up, individual pieces, and show running-time are reviewed.
- Problem scripts/beats are reworked.
- Performance notes are given in detail.
- The cast should concentrate on pacing and flow during performances.

The preview performances must be viewed as "opening night" in terms of preparation. This week is critical because, by the end of the week, the show should be in final form (line-up and major edits complete). After each preview performance, the line-up and individual pieces are reviewed and changed. Show running-time is considered heavily in the review and cut choices. The show line-up should be in final shape by the last performance of preview week. This week we concentrate on reworking individual sketches. Also, individual performance notes are given in detail.

Opening Night
This is when we bring our product to market. It is a night filled with stress and excitement. The most important part of the performance is to infuse a sense of "play" and "mischief." The cast must be reminded that they are on the BNW stage because they are incredibly talented and very funny. They must simply be themselves!

Where Do I Go From Here?
The path to innovation is a long, patient, inward journey. Remember, at the core of the Brave New Workshop is a group of individuals who have traveled down the path to their most creative self. Most of our work and products are created through an ensemble method, but like any ensemble, we are no better than any individual ensemble member. For our ensemble to be innovative, we must first be innovative individuals.

Although much of what has been discussed in this book has been in terms of ensembles and groups and classes, it is important to note that every secret we share is easily applied to you as an individual. Say yes to yourself more, defer judgment in your own thoughts, realize that, like an improv scene, everything you need in your life truly already exists and is accessible to you.

Here are some practical exercises you can use to help embrace your own sense of creativity and innovation.

1. Honestly keep track of how many times you say yes to your own (or others') ideas and how many times you say no.
2. Seek out and appreciate innovative experiences in art, business, science, and nature.
3. Begin to participate in things you are uncomfortable with, things that scare you.
4. Watch kids play.
5. Announce at the next class you lead, that for the first 15 percent of the class, no one is allowed to judge any ideas generated.
6. Ask the students you lead to let you know how they are most comfortable communicating their ideas to you and to the group.
7. Record the symptoms you experience when you are feeling comfortable and creative, and conversely, how you feel when you're frustrated and unproductive. Try to increase the number of times you experience the positive symptoms.
8. Go through the funnel process by yourself with something risk-free. For example, write a fictitious 30-second TV commercial; brainstorm the title and create an outline for your first screenplay; rewrite an epic drama as a children's book; create a sitcom in which all the characters are drawn from your own family; write your own obituary; rewrite the song lyrics to your favorite song; plan your future summer vacations by starting with, for example, "100 places I could go" and then listing key elements for each place, narrowing your choices via the funnel process.
9. Use the funnel process to write a short play, a short story, or a poem.
10. Enroll in an improv class.

11. Make a list of uncommon and unpredicted events that have resulted in innovative successes in your classroom or at home. Identify what mistakes have led to innovation.
12. Have a conversation with someone without simultaneously preparing for your reply. Challenge yourself to do absolutely *nothing* but focus on the person you're listening to and try to remember every single word they say.
13. Ask the people in your ensemble to communicate what they think is the worst possible outcome for a creative project, and then let them know that it is okay if that happens.
14. Change the channel on your TV without the remote control for one night and remember how ridiculous (and impossible) the idea of a wireless remote control must have seemed in 1978.
15. Ask your students to attempt to create a leaderless class for the day, and then invite a stranger to join you for that class. See if the stranger can identify the leader of your group.

You can use our secrets to discover your own individual style of creativity. In forty-five years of improvisation, the Brave New Workshop has witnessed what happens when people decide to take action and incorporate these principles into their lives. All of the philosophies in the world won't increase innovation or creativity until someone internalizes them and takes action. Take action!

Insights from Everyday Actors, Writers, and Teachers

We're thankful for the insights that follow. These individuals are prime examples of how practicing the Brave New Workshop secrets can positively affect your work.

> *My ability to teach seventh graders for the past twenty-three years has been enhanced by my improv training. The inherent randomness and unpredictability of adolescents tends to encourage a fluid approach to teaching. By having a relatively unscripted plan for the day, I'm able to adjust to the looniness caused by barometric changes, hormones, and post-Halloween hyperglycemia.*

Improv principles such as honesty, trust, listening, and staying "in the moment" have really helped my work and personal life. I find it easier to deal with change. Improv helps me to deal with events that don't go according to the master plan and "surprises."

Jim Kojis
Seventh Grade Teacher

When I started studying at the Brave New Institute, I had years of experience as a graphic designer and art director. I am also a trained teacher with a BFA. Improv drew my attention primarily because I had a desire to improve on my presentation skills. A friend of mine kept telling me that I should take classes with the Brave New Workshop. I thought I'd be learning how to present myself more clearly and humorously. What I learned is that improv isn't jokes or gimmicks; it's about observing, telling the truth, and playing with the results. It's a daily practice. It's a good way to live your life.

As a college design teacher, I find new students are often very attached to familiar ideas. One of my jobs is to teach them how to innovate: to create and recognize a "big idea." It was improv that actually helped me visualize that the most innovative ideas often surface from unlikely pairings of things and the willingness to create a new relationship between them.

Judith Froemming
College Design Instructor

As a college professor, studying improv has improved my work life in countless ways. Here are a few.

1. *A much stronger ability to think on my feet.*
2. *A much stronger ability to connect with undergraduates.*
3. *Better listening skills.*
4. *Greater confidence in front of the class.*
5. *An incredible new repertoire of teaching resources in terms of examples and classroom exercises.*

6. A much stronger ability to facilitate cohesion among colleagues.
7. A much stronger ability to facilitate group interactions.
8. A much greater willingness to take risks.
9. Most important, a tendency to see the workplace as a positive, playful environment in which colleagues may enjoy each other's company without losing productivity.

Studying improvisation is important for anyone interested in personal or professional growth. I cannot stress this enough. One does not have to be "a ham" or love the spotlight to be a good improviser. In fact, those who think they're funny often are in for a rude awakening when they've got to learn to share the spotlight with others, or even sacrifice their own "glory" for the success of the group. One can participate at any age or skill level—emphasis is placed on spontaneity, listening, and working with others rather than on one's individual ability to make others laugh.

Bernard Armada, PhD
Chair & Assistant Professor
Communication Studies Department,
University of St. Thomas

Some graduates of the Brave New Institute (BNI) recently provided the following insights in response to how their improv training has helped them in their careers.

How has the BNW writing process helped you with your sketch writing and/or other writing?

Using the key elements helps make sure that an idea that I come up with actually has some wings to it. I have found that using key elements first ensure the ideas and relationships are actually strong enough before I start writing the dialogue.

C. Colin Cox,
Writer; actor; leader of Twin Cities comedy
writing group; member of Six Ring Circus;
day job, communications coordinator

The key elements form is helpful because it forces the writer to discover what the essence of the scene is. Boiling it down to its basic elements gives the writer a clear vision for what s/he is writing. It's like laying out a map for where you are going, and then the writing process itself is like taking the trip and discovering new things along the way.

Corey Mills,
Actor, dancer, and dance instructor; BNI instructor

It really has become a map from which I work off of in order to heighten scenes. When we improv scenes for the Brave New Others, I am able to put what was said and done on stage into a format that tells me important aspects of that scene. From there I am able to generate a discussion with the cast that is more focused on what can heighten that particular scene.

David Kappelhoff,
Teacher/counselor for at-risk adolescents;
BNI instructor; director of Brave New Others

I think I am a much more confident writer. Previously, I was one of those writers who wrote their first draft without much thought or focus. Then I would spend a lot of time second-guessing my instincts. The key element process has helped me really refine my ability to put my ideas on paper, and then to write drafts confidently. In addition, it has given me the focus to explore ideas that I normally would have abandoned.

As a teacher, it has made me a much better teacher of writing. I am able to bring in writing samples that I am proud to model. But it has also given me a better understanding of how to take a student's idea and help them find the best way to bring that idea to fruition.

Beth Dickey,
Writer; performer; elementary school teacher

Practical Applications

It has helped focus students who are new to the writing process and helped them get their original ideas out without losing them or having them get muddled along the way.

Mike Fotis,
Writer/actor; member of the BNW
mainstage ensemble and of the highly acclaimed
improv group, Ferrari-McSpeedy

Through the writing process, I can identify the difference between a funny premise or "bit" compared to a full fledge sketch—one with not only a funny character or joke, but a strong satirical point as well.

Kristine Kvanli,
On-air host for ShoppingSource.com,
Tina from *Tony & Tina's Wedding*,
instructor for BNI youth performance teams

The structure allows you to lay out the main action, the satirical point, etc. In so doing, you can quickly assess weaknesses and strengths within the scene before you even write it. Not only does that save time, but it helps you learn why things are funny, why sketches are successful, etc.

Lauren Anderson,
BNW mainstage actor/writer;
BNI instructor

At first I was intimidated about sketch writing, wondering how I was going to turn my ideas into sketches. However, once I worked my ideas into a key element, the sketches just emerged. I think the key element is an amazingly effective way to write good sketches.

Jessie Welsch,
Real estate agent;
part-time actor

The key element process gave me a direction to go in and also to concentrate on the components of a sketch to organize my ideas.

It also helped in the editing and creation process because it gave specific categories to look at in terms of what might need more work or what was missing altogether in a particular sketch.

John Haynes, Director of the BNI;
full-time actor/writer/director

It allows the writer to bring an idea to the group and say, "Here's what I have so far. I'm a little stumped about where I want to go next. I think the premise is good but I'd like to get some input as to how to round out the rest of the sketch." With any group of writers, each creative mind brings a little something different to the table. Some people are great at writing characters; some are great at writing dialogue; some are great at developing plot-lines; and some are great at tying everything together. It allows a team of writers to easily collaborate on a sketch idea by harnessing the group's natural chemistry. It also keeps the writer honest and focused. I, personally, have continued to reference the key elements document when writing sketches for the BNW as well as when writing sketches for personal projects outside of the Workshop.

Doug Aamoth,
Computer technician and website designer;
video production artist;
Brave New Others alumni;
performer with the Six Ring Circus

How has your understanding of the eight secrets helped you become a better writer and/or performer?

I have found that there is a surprising amount of power in accepting all ideas. As a writer, accepting all ideas means that I have discovered new ideas for making a scene work and that two seemingly different scenes can find themselves inter-linked. Ignoring things would have eliminated these wonderful discoveries.

C. Colin Cox

For me, two stand out among the eight: "accepting all ideas" and "deferring judgment." The students I've seen who've made the most progress are the ones who learn to stop judging themselves (if they stop judging themselves first, it is easier for them to stop judging others) and who accept their own ideas as valid (which of course involves creative risk taking). Deferring judgment and accepting ideas are like the foundation of a house. If the foundation is strong, the rest of the house will be good; but without it, the house will either look funny or fall down.

Corey Mills

Accepting all ideas and deferring judgment have become the strongest tools for me when writing a script. Accepting all ideas gets me started and out of my head, and deferring judgment gets me to add things to the script until I've exhausted all resources. I use this to teach kids at school how to begin their writing. I tell them to just write whatever comes first to their minds, and not to judge it. So many kids at school are paralyzed by a blank page and they are thinking, "Crap, this has to be perfect!" so I come in and just keep saying, "Just write. Don't judge. The process is the perfection."

David Kappelhoff

The 8 secrets have really helped me to find a voice. They helped me break out my safety zone and take chances. I am writing better and saying yes to ideas and relationships I never would have before. I am fully exploring the potential of every idea I have before I move on to something else.

Beth Dickey

Deferring judgment is a big one, especially in the first cast meeting when we toss out ideas for the show's theme and sketches. Cast members have to be open to that process and to others' ideas, or the whole thing falls apart. It also rather quickly teaches cast members the idea of constructive, as opposed to destructive, criticism.

Mike Fotis

As an actor/writer and instructor, the 8 secrets have become a philosophy, not a guideline. During development of a show with five or six other actor/writers, the secrets are a wonderful facilitator for creativity, and the best, most practical way of creating support and honor in the "group."

Kristine Kvanli

Saying yes to new ideas is a huge reason sketches are successful. I was eating dinner at Chipotle before a BNW rehearsal for the Christmas show, and all of a sudden an idea came to me... Burrito Jesus! Perfect! I ran into rehearsal that night and pitched my idea to the cast. Instead of dismissing my idea as ridiculous, they asked me to write some key elements for it. Because they said yes to a rather silly idea, we were able to go from me shouting "You know! Burrito Jesus! Get it?!" to a successful blackout scene in the show.

Lauren Anderson

Practicing "yes, and," creative risk taking, and making declarations helped me to think outside the box and has taken my creative thinking to a different level.

Jessie Welsch

As a writer, making declarations is crucial because in the process of writing scripts for a particular show or event it is necessary to be clear and bold in my communication to the client or director as to what the intentions of the script are.

John Haynes

What are some things about BNI training that have helped you in the realm of writing, performing, improvising, auditioning, or directing?

As an improviser and actor, I've learned to take chances. It's easy for me to play an old grumpy grandpa or an overexcited child, but it's more of a challenge (and more fun!) to suddenly find myself embodying a father embarrassed by his son's lack of social skills, or a pathetic White rapper.

C. Colin Cox

I've learned to listen more and to keep my point of view while doing this. As a director I'm not trying to ram my ideas down people's heads, but I'm able to incorporate my ideas with others' ideas and create wonderful scripts. Also, as a director I've learned how to develop a statusless environment so that all ideas are accepted from the cast, including the tech and music directors' ideas. The goal is always to work together by taking care of yourself.

David Kappelhoff

The training helped me explore improvisation on a whole new level, and it broke down my preconceived notions about improvisation. The teachers caused me to take a look at my habits and my comfort zones, and worked to push me past them. Ultimately, I am a better improviser because of this training.

Beth Dickey

It helps me declare often and declare big. The BNI has taught me that I have to make my intentions known—DECLARE my ideas, excitement, hopes, concerns, etc. I have gotten jobs just by declaring my desires—declaring my confidence and declaring my passion for a project or a particular role. I would have never done that without learning the art of DECLARATION.

Kristine Kvanli

The most, I think, is instant adaptability. I have become rather quick at changing speeds, characters, focus, energy, etc. This allows me to generate ideas and implement them without a lot of processing time. The time I save in processing and decompressing, I use to generate more ideas!

Lauren Anderson

Having the BNI's improv classes on my acting resume has opened up doors for me, as directors in the Twin Cities respect the BNW and the actors and writers who have studied with them. I truly believe that the BNI launched my acting career and for that I will always be grateful!

Jessie Welsch

My level of confidence to audition increased. As a director it has given me a keen eye for the stage picture for every scene, and has helped me to live in that statusless environment so that I am open to the feedback of others in the show and using the collective creativity of the cast.

John Haynes

In the case of writing, the BNI taught me to write with a purpose in mind. Instead of writing something and saying, "This is funny," the BNI teaches you to question yourself as a writer. "Why is this scene funny? Why are these people here and why are the things that they're saying funny? What are they like as characters and how will the audience identify with them?" As a local actor, I love going to auditions now. Even if I'm sent to an audition for a part that I might not be "right for," I've been confident enough in front of casting agents and directors that they're now asking for me by name for other parts that come up in the future.

Also, I think that to dramatic actors, in general, there's kind of a stigma that doing improv is kind of "hacky" or is kind of a step backwards as far as training goes. I would implore those that say that to take a year of training at the BNI and see if they don't come away from the school far more enriched and enlightened.

Doug Aamoth

Appendix 1
A Form to Organize the Key Elements of Your Sketch

This document is called "Sketch Worksheet Form" on your CD

BRAVE NEW WORKSHOP SKETCH WORKSHEET
A Form to Organize the Key Elements of Your Sketch
The purpose of this worksheet is:

1. to give you a format for organizing and recording the key elements of your sketch;
2. to ensure you have a very thorough list of key elements by giving you questions to answer and points to defend; and
3. to prepare you for the "filling in the blank with dialogue" step of the sketch-writing process.

There are two important pieces of information to include for each of the five key elements: the simple facts (often short or one-word factual answers), and the feel of the key element (usually a few sentences of description that get to the core truth of this key element). Please be sure your answers address both the facts and the feel when completing this form!

1. The Satirical Point
   a) In a word or two, what is the basic topic of this sketch?
   b) In a sentence, what is the point you are making with this sketch? (i.e., What is your opinion? If you could have the audience walk

away with a one-sentence summary of your point, what would that one sentence be?)
c) In a few sentences, describe the satirical point you are making and why you are making it. Include comments on why you think this deserves stage time, why it is an important point to make, the flavor or feel that you would like this sketch to have, and what reaction you'd like to get.

2. The Characters

For each character in your sketch, complete the following two sections:

a) List factual data on this character that is important to this sketch. This factual data might include (but is not limited to) age, occupation, sexual orientation, marital status, ethnic or religious background, physical characteristics, recent events in life, etc.
b) Also, describe the point of view and the bottom line of this character. In a few sentences, you should be able to give a very clear idea of what this character is about; what makes them tick; what opinions, attitudes, and characteristics of this character will most impact how they behave in this scene? Which side of the satirical point does this person represent? What is this person's role in this sketch (main character, ambiance, comic relief, etc.)? What is this person trying to accomplish in this scene? How would you describe this person to a friend if you were gossiping about him/her?

Character Name: _____
Age: _____
Occupation: _____
Sexual orientation/Marital Status: _____
Ethnic background/geographic orientation: _____
Important physical characteristics: _____
Recent historical events in his/her life: _____
Other: _____
Describe his/her point of view: _____

3. The Action of the Scene

a) In one sentence, describe what this scene is about—what will happen in this scene?
b) Describe the overall feel, style, rhythm, or pace of this scene.
c) List the major events or beats that will occur from beginning to end in this scene. This should be a sort of play-by-play of what the characters do in the scene. This can take the form of beginning, middle, and end, if that is helpful.

4. The Environment, Location, or Setting

a) List the important factual data that describes the setting or location of this scene. This factual data might include (but is not limited to) year, day of the week, time of the day, country, state, city, specific physical location, set pieces, important props or costumes, tone, temperature, mood, colors, etc.
b) Take some time to visualize the setting in your mind, and then describe the setting as if you were describing it to a blind person, with the goal of describing the feel of the setting, more than just the factual elements.

5. The "Funny"

Write an explanation of why you think this scene will be funny, and where you think the opportunities for humor exist. Is it the premise that is funny? Will the characters be funny? Will it be visual gags? Is it the characters in an odd setting that makes it funny? Why did it make you laugh? What made you think this would be funny?

Copyright, Brave New Workshop Theatre, 1999

Appendix 2
Sample Sketch, From Key Elements through Final Sketch

The following text provides an example of one sketch, from its key elements through several iterations and, finally, its final draft, which was used in performance. Although the path of a sketch is never the same, I chose this one because it demonstrates a pretty typical journey from a simple point of view and idea to the final stage version of a sketch. I also chose it because I believe it represents great satire.

Brave New Workshop Theatre

DATE: 7/26/00
SHOW: Dull Man Running
TITLE: "Tiger!"
DRAFT: Key Elements—1
WRITERS: S. Wexler

Satirical Point:
You can still be a racist even if you're clueless.

Characters:
Susan Plunkett: a young white woman who fancies herself a liberal-minded intellectual. Susan sells Pampered Chef and has tons of friends who look like her. Married with 2 kids.

Action:
Susan explains why she is not a racist because of her love for Tiger Woods.

Environment:
Susan's living room.

Funny:
Susan believes that she is truly not a racist but proves countless times throughout her speech that she is.

Brave New Workshop Theatre

DATE: 7/27/00
SHOW: Dull Man Running
TITLE: "Tiger!"
DRAFT: Key Elements—2A
WRITERS: S. Wexler

Satirical Point:
You can still be a racist even if you're clueless.

Characters:

Morton Grazer: School Board President. 53 years old, white, married with 2 kids in college. Morton has lived in Apple Valley for 25 years. Morton has a comb-over.

Susan Plunkett: a young white woman who fancies herself a liberal-minded intellectual. Susan sells Pampered Chef and has tons of friends who look like her. Married with 2 kids.

Jan Nelson: School Board Member. She's a retired gym teacher.

School Board Members: See Southdale Mall on a Saturday for inspiration.

Action:
- Opens on school board meeting with closing of benign school issue

- Next issue is introduced: urban exchange program with inner city school
- School board member asks what the program is—general uneasiness throughout the room
- Morton briefly describes the proposed day-long program: Apple Valley kids will go to Minneapolis North High and vice versa.
- Issue is opened up for debate
- Susan launches into a speech about her affinity for black people and culture, basing her argument on her love for Tiger Woods
- Morton asks for clarification: "So you are in favor of an urban exchange?"
- Susan says "No, but not because they're black"

Environment:
School Board meeting at Apple Valley Middle School Library.

Funny:
Susan believes that she is truly not a racist but proves countless times throughout her speech that she is. Reveal at the end will also be funny because it will expose her even more.

Brave New Workshop Theatre

DATE: 7/28/00
SHOW: Dull Man Running
TITLE: "Tiger!"
DRAFT: Key Elements—2B—Rewrite with new setting
WRITERS: S. Wexler

Satirical Point:
You can still be a racist even if you're clueless.

Characters:
Susan Plunkett: a young white woman who fancies herself a liberal-minded intellectual. Susan sells Pampered Chef and has tons of friends who look like her. Married with 2 kids.

Jan Nelson: Susan's neighbor for 12 years. Jan is also married with a little girl. Jan watches Martha Stewart everyday and makes her own greeting cards for every occasion.

Action:
- Susan finds Jan in her backyard; gives her Pampered Chef order
- Susan informs Jan that she is moving "closer to the cities" and says that she is not open to living in "various neighborhoods" in the Minneapolis area
- Silence as Susan begins to feel uncomfortable about her veiled statement
- Susan explains that she is not a racist because of her love for Tiger Woods, et al.
- Jan asks her if Susan is moving to Minneapolis and Susan says "No! But it's not because they are black."

Environment:
Jan's backyard. Jan is gardening.

Funny:
Susan believes that she is truly not a racist but proves countless times throughout her speech that she is.

Brave New Workshop Theatre

DATE: 7/30/00
SHOW: Dull Man Running
TITLE: "Tiger"
DRAFT: 1A
WRITERS: S. Wexler

Premise:
Clueless suburban school board member reveals her ignorance and racist beliefs in an emotional testimony regarding an urban exchange with a Minneapolis high school.

Setting:
School board meeting at Apple Valley Middle School library in Apple Valley.

Characters:
Susan Plunkett: a young white woman who fancies herself a liberal-minded intellectual. Susan sells Pampered Chef and has tons of friends who look like her. Married with 3 kids.

Morton Grazer: School board president. 53 years old, white, married with 2 kids in college. Morton has lived in Apple Valley for 25 years. Morton has a comb-over.

Jan Nelson: School board member for 12 years. She's a retired gym teacher.

(Lights up on school board meeting.)

MORTON
Alrightee then! It looks like the teacher's lounge will get a new microwave. I'll get the ball moving on that one. *(shifts uncomfortably)* Now . . . it seems that, uh, we have one more action item on our list today. As you know, the school board must approve all educational programs, outreach opportunities and the like, and since we're the school board, I thought it would be appropriate that we *(falters)* . . . do just that. *(tries to lighten mood)* Ha, ha! Since we're the school board! *(no response)* Alrightee then! This action item is real different. It's been proposed that the Apple Valley school district—that's us!—do an *(starts reading from notes)* urban exchange with some schools over there in Minneapolis. *(pause)* So, okay, let's vote! All opposed—

JAN
(suspiciously) Whoa! What is an "urban exchange" exactly?

MORTON
Yeah, that's a good question, real helpful. *(reading from notes)* "An urban exchange will challenge suburban and metropolitan schools alike to participate in a learning operative meant to bridge cultural and educational differences along diverse lines of color, race, and creed."

(Silence)

JAN
Okay, I'm confused. What is this, Morton? You said "exchange" in there somewhere. What are we exchanging?

MORTON
Uh . . . students, students.

JAN
Exchange them for what?

MORTON
Other students.

JAN
Students from Minneapolis?

MORTON
Yes! *(reading)* Minneapolis North, Roosevelt—that's where Governor Ventura went, I might add . . . Yes, so the students come here . . .

JAN
(finally getting it). They come here?

MORTON
(giving in) Yes, they come here.

JAN
(as if talking through a difficult math problem) And we send our students . . .

MORTON
Over there. *(with tired enthusiasm)* But, only for a day each semester.

(Silence as this sinks in)

SUSAN
(clearing throat) Well, this is exciting. I think. Don't you think? Yes, very, very exciting. Morton, I'd like to share now, if I may *(Morton nods weakly and sits down).* I'd like to share that I think this is

exciting and different. Minneapolis schools are very rich in diversity and I am not a racist. In fact, I love black people. I really, really do. I love that Tiger Woods. I think he is so . . . wonderful and . . . just wonderful. *(starts getting revved up)* I'd invite him in my home, that's how wonderful I think he is. I wish he were mine. This is how much I love Tiger Woods—I would trade one of my own sons for Tiger. Tiger, in addition to being a world-class athlete and Nike spokesman is actually multi-ethnic, so it goes without saying that I also love Asian peoples and other kinds of peoples as well. I love Asian cooking, which is a very important part of their culture. I would rather eat a Szechwan Chicken Lean Cuisine than spaghetti or something more Western. You all know that I've hosted many diverse students in my home. Bjorn and Greta were very ethnic and so different. They didn't speak English very well. They could have been black—I wouldn't have noticed. Let's just say, I'm comfortable with them—with those people, uh . . . I don't even notice color. I'm colorblind, really. Colorblind! All I see is white! I watch Oprah every day and I forget she's black. Absolutely forget! I read Toni Morrison's *The Bluest Eye* with Oprah and that is a story about a girl who is black. And that Halle Berry, you know her, right? An African American actress—so beautiful. I mean she looks white! I would love to be as pretty as Halle Berry. And Tiger is so handsome, too.

(Susan sits. Silence. Scattered claps.)

MORTON

Thank you, Susan. Okay, so you are in favor of an urban exchange?

SUSAN

Oh, no! No! My boys are in sports and I wouldn't want them to miss any—and those Minneapolis students, I'm sure, are real busy, so—I think they should stay there. For now. *(pause)* But, it's not because they're black.

(Blackout or transition.)

Copyright Brave New Workshop, 2000

Brave New Workshop Theatre

DATE: 7/31/00
SHOW: Dull Man Running
TITLE: "Tiger"
DRAFT: 1B—with new backyard setting
WRITERS: S. Wexler

Premise:
Clueless woman reveals her ignorance and racist beliefs.

Setting:
Jan Nelson's backyard in Apple Valley.

Characters:

Susan Plunkett: a young white woman who fancies herself a liberal-minded intellectual. Susan sells Pampered Chef and has tons of friends who look like her. Married with 3 kids.

Jan Nelson: Susan's neighbor for 12 years. Jan is also married with a little girl. Jan watches Martha Stewart everyday and makes her own greeting cards for every occasion.

(Lights up on Susan crossing the yard to Jan. Jan is working in her garden.)

SUSAN

(handing bag to Jan) Jan! Hi! Here's your Pampered Chef order. The food chopper is in there and the pizza baking stone, garlic press. Oh, and I also threw in some of those corn-cob holders.

JAN

Oh, great, thanks! I've been waiting for this stuff!

SUSAN

(glancing down) Your garden looks great!

JAN

Thanks, thanks. Yeah, it's coming along. *(pause)* Say, did I hear right that you and Bill are moving?

SUSAN

(slightly embarrassed) Yes . . . I've been meaning to tell you, but it's been crazy around the house. We've had three offers already and it's not even on the market!

JAN

Wow! So, where are you looking?

SUSAN

Well, Bill wants to move closer to the city.

JAN

Oh.

SUSAN

Yeah, he's tired of the commute and, you know, he wants to take advantage of the hot housing market.

JAN

Well, sure, sure. I'm just so sad to see you go. *(pause)* So, You're looking in the cities?

SUSAN

(adamant) Near the Cities. Near. Our realtor wanted us to look . . . in Minneapolis at various neighborhoods and, well, that's a mixed bag. I mean, some of those neighborhoods can get a little . . . well, it's just real different from here.

JAN

Oh sure, yeah.

(Silence)

SUSAN

(in a rush) I mean . . . I don't mean to sound . . . I am not one of those racist people. I am not a racist. In fact, I love . . . black people and black culture . . . I really, really do. I love that Tiger Woods. I think he is so . . . wonderful and . . . just wonderful. *(starts getting revved up)* I'd invite him in my home, that's how wonderful I think he is. I wish he were mine. This is how much I love Tiger Woods—I would trade one of my own sons for Tiger. You know I

was reading that Tiger, in addition to being a world-class athlete and Nike spokesman, is actually multi-ethnic, so it goes without saying that I also love Asian peoples and other kinds of peoples as well. I love Asian cooking, which is a very important part of their culture. I love those Szechwan Chicken Lean Cuisines even more than . . . spaghetti or something more Western. Let's just say, I'm comfortable with them—with those people, uh . . . I don't even notice color. I'm colorblind, really. Colorblind! All I see is white! I watch Oprah every day and I forget she's black. Absolutely forget! I read Toni Morrison's *The Bluest Eye* with Oprah and that is a story about a girl who is black. Sometimes—and I'm not kidding here—I wish I was black so that I could marry a black man. Oh, and that Halle Berry, you know her, right? An African American actress—so beautiful. I mean she looks white! I would love to be as pretty as Halle Berry. And Tiger is so handsome, too.

(Silence as Jan stares at her)

JAN

(a bit confused) So. you're moving to Minneapolis?

SUSAN

Oh, no! No! *(pause)* But, it's not because they're black.

(Blackout or transition.)

Copyright Brave New Workshop, 2000

Brave New Workshop Theatre

DATE: 8/02/00
SHOW: Dull Man Running
TITLE: "Tiger!"
DRAFT: 2—School Board Setting
WRITERS: S. Wexler

Premise:
Clueless suburban school board member reveals her ignorance and racist beliefs in an emotional testimony regarding an urban exchange with a Minneapolis high school.

Setting:
School board meeting at Apple Valley Middle School library in Apple Valley.

Characters:
Susan Plunkett: a young white woman who fancies herself a liberal-minded intellectual. Susan sells Pampered Chef and has tons of friends who look like her. Married with 3 kids.

Morton Grazer: School board president. 53 years old, white, married with 2 kids in college. Morton has lived in Apple Valley for 25 years. Morton has a comb-over.

Jan Nelson: School board member for 12 years. She's a retired gym teacher.

(Lights up on school board meeting.)

MORTON
Alrightee then! It looks like the teacher's lounge will get a new microwave. I'll get the ball moving on that one. *(shifts uncomfortably)* Now . . . it seems that, uh, we have one more action item on our list today and, uh, I think we all know how we feel about this one. Yeah, this action item is real different. It's been proposed that the Apple Valley school district—that's us—do an *(starts reading from notes)* urban exchange with some schools over there in Minneapolis. *(pause)* So, okay, let's vote! All opposed—

JAN
(Suspiciously) Whoa! What is an "urban exchange" exactly?

MORTON
Yeah, that's a good question, real helpful. *(reading from notes)* "An urban exchange will challenge suburban and metropolitan schools alike to participate in a learning operative meant to bridge cultural and educational differences along diverse lines of color, race, and creed."

(Silence)

JAN
Okay, I'm confused. What is this Morton? You said "exchange" in there somewhere. What are we exchanging?

MORTON
Uh . . . students, students.

JAN
Exchange them for what?

MORTON
Other students.

JAN
Students from Minneapolis?

MORTON
Yes! (reading) Minneapolis North, Roosevelt—that's where Governor Ventura went, I might add . . . Yes, so the students come here . . .

JAN
(finally getting it) They come here?

MORTON
(giving in) Yes, they come here.

JAN
(as if talking through a difficult math problem) And we send our students . . .

MORTON
Over there. *(with tired enthusiasm)* But, only for a day each semester. So, any discussion . . . *(as if expecting)* Susan?

SUSAN
(already standing—seems surprised that she's been called on so quickly) Oh, well! Good! Here I am! *(pause)* Well, this is exciting. I think. Don't you think? Yes, very, very exciting. I'd like to share that I think this is exciting and different. Minneapolis schools are very rich in diversity and that's a good thing. I am not one of those racist people. I am not a racist. In fact, I love black people. I really, really do. I love that Tiger Woods. I think he is so . . . wonderful and . . .

just wonderful. *(starts getting revved up)* I'd invite him in my home, that's how wonderful I think he is. I wish he were mine. This is how much I love Tiger Woods—I would trade one of my own sons for Tiger. I was reading that Tiger, in addition to being a world-class athlete and Nike spokesman, is actually multi-ethnic, so it goes without saying that I also love Asian peoples and other kinds of peoples as well. I love Asian cooking, which is a very important part of their culture. I love those Szechwan Chicken Lean Cuisines even more than spaghetti or something more Western. Let's just say, I'm comfortable with them—with those people . . . All people . . . okay, I don't even notice color. I'm colorblind, really. Colorblind! All I see is white! I watch Oprah every day and I forget she's black. Absolutely forget! I read Toni Morrison's *The Bluest Eye* with Oprah and that is a story about a girl who is black. Sometimes—and I'm not kidding here—I wish I was black so that I could marry a black man. And that Halle Berry, you know her, right? An African American actress—so beautiful. I mean she looks white! I would love to be as pretty as Halle Berry. And Tiger is so handsome, too.

(Susan sits. Silence. Scattered claps.)

MORTON
Thank you, Susan. Okay, so you are in favor of inner city kids coining to our school?

SUSAN
Oh, no! No! But, it's not because they're black.

(Blackout or transition.)

Copyright Brave New Workshop, 2000

Brave New Workshop Theatre

DATE: 08/06/00
SHOW: Dull Man Running
TITLE: "Tiger!"
DRAFT: 3
WRITERS: S. Wexler

Premise:
Clueless suburban school board member reveals her ignorance and racist beliefs in an emotional testimony regarding an urban exchange with a Minneapolis high school.

Setting:
School board meeting at Apple Valley Middle School library in Apple Valley.

Characters:
Susan Plunkett: a young white woman who fancies herself a liberal-minded intellectual. Susan sells Pampered Chef and has tons of friends who look like her. Married with 3 kids.

Morton Grazer: School board president. 53 years old, white, married with 2 kids in college. Morton has lived in Apple Valley for 25 years. Morton has a comb-over.

Jan Nelson: School board member for 12 years. She's a retired gym teacher.

Various school board members.

(Lights up on school board meeting.)

MORTON
Alrightee then! It looks like the teacher's lounge will get a new microwave. I'll get the ball moving on that one. *(shifts uncomfortably)* Now . . . it seems that, uh, we have one more action item on our list today and, uh, I think we all know how we feel about this one. Yeah, this action item is real different. It's been proposed that the Apple Valley school district—that's us!—do an *(starts reading from notes)* urban exchange with some schools over there in Minneapolis. *(pause)* So, okay, let's vote! All opposed—

JAN
(Suspiciously) Whoa! What is an "urban exchange" exactly?

MORTON

Yeah, that's a good question, Jan. Real helpful. *(reading from notes)* "an urban exchange will challenge suburban and metropolitan schools alike to participate in a learning operative meant to bridge cultural arid educational differences along diverse lines of color, race, and creed."

(Silence)

JAN

Okay, I'm confused. What is this, Morton? You said "exchange" in there somewhere. What are we exchanging?

MORTON

Uh . . . students, students.

JAN

Exchange them for what?

MORTON

Other students.

JAN

Students from Minneapolis?

MORTON

Yes!

JAN

(getting it) Oh, Lord!

MORTON

(reading) Students from Minneapolis North, Roosevelt—that's where Governor Ventura went, I might add *(no response from board)* . . . Yes, so the students come here and we send ours . . . over there. *(with tired enthusiasm)* So, any discussion . . . *(as if expecting)* Susan?

SUSAN

(already standing—seems surprised that she's been called an so quickly) Oh, well! Good! Here I am! *(pause)* Well, this is exciting.

I think. Don't you think? Yes, very, very exciting. *(for Jan's benefit)* I'd like to share that I think this is exciting and different. Minneapolis schools are very rich in diversity and that's a good thing. I am not one of those racist people. I am not a racist. In fact, I love black people. I really, really do. I love that Tiger Woods. I think he is so . . . wonderful and . . . just wonderful. *(starts getting revved up)* I'd invite him in my home, that's how wonderful I think he is. I wish he were mine. I would trade one of my own sons for Tiger—that's how much I love black people! Let's just say, I'm comfortable with them, with those people . . . All people! . . . Okay, I don't even notice color. I'm colorblind, really. Colorblind! All I see is white! I watch Oprah every day and I forget she's black. Absolutely forget! I read Toni Morrison's *The Bluest Eye* with Oprah and that is a story about a girl who is black. And that Halle Berry, you know her, right? An African American actress—so beautiful. She looks white! I would love to be as pretty as Halle Berry. And Tiger is just so wonderful, too.

(Susan sits. Silence. Scattered claps.)

MORTON

Thank you, Susan. Okay, so you are in favor of inner city kids coming to our school?

SUSAN

Oh, no! No! But, it's not because they're black.

(Blackout or transition.)

Copyright Brave New Workshop, 2000

Brave New Workshop Theatre

DATE: 08/23/00
SHOW: Dull Man Running
TITLE: "Tiger!"
DRAFT: Final
WRITERS: S. Wexler

Premise:
Clueless suburban school board member reveals her ignorance and racist beliefs in an emotional testimony regarding an urban exchange with a Minneapolis high school.

Setting:
School board meeting at Apple Valley Middle School library in Apple Valley.

Characters:
Susan Plunkett: a young white woman who fancies herself a liberal-minded intellectual. Susan sells Pampered Chef and has tons of friends who look like her. Married with 3 kids.

Morton Grazer: School board president. 53 years old, white, married with 2 kids in college. Morton has lived in Apple Valley for 25 years. Morton has a comb-over.

Jan Nelson: School board member for 12 years. She's a retired gym teacher.

Various school board members.

(Lights up on school board meeting.)

MORTON
Alrightee then! It looks like the teacher's lounge will get a new microwave. I'll inform the Apple Valley Lounge Boosters to move forward on that one. *(shifts uncomfortably)* Now . . . it seems that, uh, we have one more action item on our list today and, uh, I think we all know how we feel about this one. Yeah, this action item is real different. It's been proposed that the Apple Valley school district—that's us!—do an *(starts reading from notes)* urban exchange with some schools over there in Minneapolis. So, okay, let's vote! All opposed—

JAN
(suspiciously) Whoa! What is an "urban exchange" exactly?

MORTON

Yes, that's a good question, Jan. Real helpful. *(reading from notes)* "An urban exchange will challenge suburban and metropolitan schools alike to participate in a learning operative meant to bridge cultural and educational differences along diverse lines of color, race, and creed."

(Silence)

JAN

Okay, I'm confused. What is this Morton? You said "exchange" in there somewhere. What are we exchanging?

MORTON

Uh . . . students, students.

JAN

Exchange them for what?

MORTON

Other students.

JAN

Students from Minneapolis?

MORTON

Yes!

JAN

(getting it) Oh, Lord!

MORTON

(reading) Students from Minneapolis North, Roosevelt—that's where Governor Ventura went, I might add *(no response from board)* . . . So, any discussion . . . *(as if expecting)* Susan?

SUSAN

(already standing—seems surprised that she's been called on so quickly) Oh, well! Good! Here I am! *(pause)* Well, this is exciting. I think. Don't you think? Yes, very, very exciting. I'd like to share that I think this is exciting and different. Minneapolis schools are very rich in diversity and that's a good thing. I am not one of those

racist people. I am not a racist. In fact, I love black people. I really, really do. I love that Tiger Woods. I think he is so . . . wonderful and . . . just wonderful. *(starts getting revved up)* I'd invite him in my home, that's how wonderful I think he is. I wish he were mine. I would trade one of my own sons for Tiger—that's how much I love black people! Let's just say, I'm comfortable with them, with those people . . . All people! . . . Okay, I don't even notice color. I'm colorblind, really. Colorblind! All I see is white! I watch Oprah every day and I forget she's black. Absolutely forget! And that Halle Berry, you know her, right? An African American actress—so beautiful. I mean, she looks white! I would love to be as pretty as Halle Berry. And Tiger is just so wonderful, too.

(Susan sits. Silence. Scattered claps.)

MORTON
Thank you, Susan. Okay, so, just to clarify, you are in favor of inner city kids coming to our school?

SUSAN
Oh, no! No!

(Blackout or transition.)

Copyright Brave New Workshop, 2000

Appendix 3
Other Sample Sketches

Brave New Workshop Theatre

DATE: 09/29/99
SHOW: Jessie Goes to Hollywood
TITLE: "Premium Arm"
DRAFT: Final
WRITERS: Cast

(Blackout Scene)
Eric walks onstage. In place of his right arm is a case of Grain Belt Premium beer. He is seemingly unaware.

VOICEOVER
We've secretly replaced Eric Nelson's arm with a case of Grain Belt Premium beer. Let's see if he notices.

Eric
Yo taxi!

Eric walks downstage and attempts to hail a cab with his beer arm. The cab goes right by.

Eric looks puzzled and a bit miffed.

VOICEOVER
Hmmm

Brave New Workshop Theatre

DATE: 09/06/00
SHOW: Dull Man Running
TITLE: "You Suck"
DRAFT: 4
WRITERS: S. Wexler

Premise:
A political debate that disintegrates into a childish spitting fight.

Setting:
Very stuffy lecture hall. The feel of the room is very formal.

Characters:
Marla Terse: 48-year-old white Democrat; B.A. from Wellesley; running for Senate. Thin-lipped.

Mike Bland: 53-year-old white Republican senator for the state of Virginia; B.A. from George Washington University. Mike wears a headband when he plays racquetball and drinks coffee like a fiend. There is always a stain on his tie.

Miriam Quip: Moderator for Senate debates; very serious, but not angry; humorless in an earnest way. Dreams of being on Minnesota Public Radio as a political correspondent.

(Lights up on both candidates and moderator in debate setting.)

MODERATOR
(quietly in mic) Welcome to the fourth in a continuing series of Senatorial debates sponsored by the League of Women Voters. I'm Miriam Quip. *(pause)* Representing the Republican Party from the state of Virginia, Senator Mike Bland. And the Democratic candidate from Virginia, State Representative Marla Terse. *(pause)* Let us begin with Senator Bland. Senator, you have fought to lower

taxes during your years in the Senate. How would you continue this if reelected?

(While Senator talks, Terse rolls her eyes, etc.)

BLAND
Taxes hold back America's prosperity. I will do everything I can to lower taxes for . . . *(Senses that Terse is mocking him; looks over uneasily.)* . . . as long as I'm in the Senate.

MODERATOR
Representative Terse? Your response?

TERSE
To lower taxes while the national debt that paid for your defense systems in the 80s continues to grow is *(Bland makes faces behind Terse's back, etc. Terse almost catches him.)* . . . is foolhardy.

BLAND
Foolhardy? I trust that the people of this country know how to handle their money.

MODERATOR
(to Terse) Response?

(Pause.)

TERSE
(to Senator) You suck.

MODERATOR
(to Terse) Could you please clarify that statement?

TERSE
Senator Bland sucks the big one.

MODERATOR
(with complete professionalism) Senator? Your response?

BLAND
Representative Terse sucks more.

MODERATOR
Representative? The Senator has stated that you suck more. Your response?

TERSE
I double-dog-dare the Senator to explain his stupid-head financial policies—or is he too much of a fatty?

MODERATOR
We have a double-dog-dare on the floor. Senator Fatty, your response?

BLAND
I know you are but what am I?

MODERATOR
(to Terse) The Senator has implied that if you are the fatty, what is he?

TERSE
You can tell him that I'm rubber and he's glue and whatever he says bounces off of me and sticks to him.

MODERATOR
Senator, given the Representative's new statements, you are once again the fatty since it bounced off the Representative's rubber . . . exterior . . . and is now sticking to you.

BLAND
At least I don't have big fat cooties!

TERSE
(quickly) Opposite Day! Opposite Day!

MODERATOR
The Senator now has cooties.

TERSE
(even quicker) Infinity plus one!

MODERATOR
It is not customary to call infinity when "opposite day" is in place.

BLAND
Yeah! Representative Terse is a big-fat-sucky-girl-dumbhead! *(Bland starts poking Terse)*

TERSE
Senator Fattybutt is touching me! *(draws imaginary line)* Tell him to stay on his side!

BLAND
(circling Terse with his finger, almost touching her) I want to make it clear that I am not touching the Representative! I am not touching the Representative! Force field! Force field!

MODERATOR
It has been noted that the Senator is indeed not touching the Representative.

TERSE
(mocking while she's slapping away his hands) "Look at me! I'm a big dork Senator!"

BLAND
Shut up! You broke the force field!

TERSE
I hate you!

(Moderator has made her way center stage, grabbing them by the ears)

MODERATOR
I'd like to thank the League of Women Voters . . . *(candidates start crying)* Stop it! I'll give you something to cry about! I'm Miriam Quip. Thank you. *(yelling at both of candidates)* Clean up this mess!

(Blackout or transition.)

Copyright Brave New Workshop, 2000

Brave New Workshop Theatre

DATE: 11/1/00
SHOW: Home for the Hostilities, Again
TITLE: "Dueling Bells"
DRAFT: Final
WRITERS: Caleb McEwen

Premise:
Salvation Army bellringers compete for donations.

Characters:
Shopper: A generous person who can't make up his/her mind.

Ringer 1: An ambitious Salvation Army bellringer.

Ringer 2: An ambitious Salvation Army bellringer.

Quasimodo: An ambitious Salvation Army bellringer with a hunchback.

Location:
Outside the Southdale Mall during the Christmas season.

(Lights up to reveal RINGER 1 ringing a mimed bell. As he mimes this action, a bell SFX is played on the piano.

SHOPPER enters, approaches RINGER 1 with the intention of giving. As she does, RINGER 2 sets up and begins to ring.

SHOPPER changes mind and heads toward RINGER 2. RINGER 1 rings emphatically. She changes her mind again.

Pattern reverses as RINGER 2 rings emphatically.

Eventually both RINGERs square off as RINGER 1 plays a riff from *West Side Story*.

RINGER 1 rings melody to "Dueling Banjoes." RINGER 2 answers. A ringing showdown occurs as the full song is played out. SHOPPER is bewildered by decision.

As ringing duel continues, QUASIMODO sets up, upstage. He reaches above his head and pulls an imaginary rope. We hear deafening cathedral bells as the two ringers stop.

SHOPPER and RINGER 1 move to drop coins in QUASIMODO's bucket as RINGER 2 flees.

(Blackout)

Copyright Brave New Workshop Theatre 2000

Brave New Workshop Theatre

DATE: 4-12-01
SHOW: Extreme Things
TITLE: Disney Toilet
DRAFT: Final
WRITERS: Katy McEwen

Premise:
When "the total experience" goes too far

Setting:
A public restroom in Disneyworld, just outside the Country Bear Jamboree

Characters:
Jill Stein: 39-year-old mother of two who has had about enough magic

Alice Jones: Harrowed woman

Toilet: Extremely happy to take your waste, possibly the voice of a Disney character

Chorus: Whitebread, clean-cut men and women who just want to sing

(Lights up on Jill in doorway, shouting outside. "It's a Small World" is playing and children are screaming in the background.)

Jill

Kids! Mommy just has to go to the restroom, and then we'll see Mickey Mouse! *(burst of screaming)* Kids! Mommy just has to tinkle!

(Jill enters the restroom. As soon as the door closes, there is a deafening silence. Alice runs screaming across the stage and out the door.)

Alice

Nooooo! Not again!

(The silence resumes as the door shuts again. Downspot appears.)

VOICEOVER

Please step into the light. The next adventure is about to begin.

Jill

I thought this was just a restroom.

VOICEOVER

At Disney, it's never just a restroom, it's an experience. *(she runs for door)* Please do not attempt to exit the ride until it has come to a complete stop. Step into the light.

(Jill steps into the light. It begins to change. The story is enacted during the voiceover.)

VOICEOVER

Long ago, in a far away land, there lived a young man who wanted nothing more than to have the love of a beautiful, ridiculously proportioned princess. But, although the young man was charming and attractive in a non-threatening way, he was poor, and had nothing to offer the king for his daughter's hand. One day, as he was digging for dirt fruit, the young man came upon a magnificent treasure the likes of which he had never seen. He took the gift to the king, and was immediately married to the princess, who looked just a little bit ethnic but still Anglo enough to pass for white. Soon after the wedding the magnificent gift disappeared, never to be seen again.

(Elaine, wearing an archaeologist hat, walks over to Jill, looking carefully at the toilet.)

Chorus 1
Dr. Wilson! Dr. Wilson! I think I've found it!

Chorus 2
(entering) My word, Elaine! You have! After lo these many years, we have finally found it! The toilet of wonders! But who? Who in all the land is worthy to christen it? You? Or You? Or could it be You?

(They shine their flashlights on Jill, cowering in a corner.)

Jill
I just need to tinkle.

Chorus 2
Today is your lucky day! Approach the toilet of wonders. Approach the toilet of wonders!

(Jill reluctantly crosses to toilet and sits as they secure the lap bar over her.)

Chorus 1
Please keep your hands and feet inside the toilet at all times.

(Music starts. Chorus enters and begins singing and dancing.)

Toilet of Wonders

Chorus
It's the toilet of wonders! The toilet of fun! Bringing toilety goodness to everyone!
t-o-i-l-e-t o-f wonders!
It's the magical toilet of fun!

Singer 1
With its porcelain so shiny, and its flusher made of chrome,

Singer 2
The minute that you take a seat you know you've found a home!

Singer 1
Its magic brought together a princess and a schlub!

Singer 2
Which goes to show what we can do if we could only love!

(Music changes abruptly into Lion King*-esque style.)*

Singer
It's the toilet of wonders!
Bringing us together!
All men united in peace!
Oh, won't you just have a seat?

Chorus
(with singer vamping insanely over them)

I can see the past,
In your glistening bowl.
Stretching into the future,
For all to behold!

Now let's all join hands!
And put our lunch behind us!
Through the toilet,
The toilet,
The toilet!
The toilet of wonders!

(Blackout)

Brave New Workshop Theatre

DATE: 2/13/04
SHOW: Das Bootylicious
TITLE: Muslim Gal
DRAFT: Final
WRITER/S: Shanan Wexler

Premise:
Woman reveals her fear and ignorance about the Muslim faith when she has to sit next to a Muslim woman on an airplane.

Setting:
Airplane.

Characters:
Cassie Libby: nice girl, really nice girl, but just doesn't "get it." Knows very little of about the Muslim faith, and is altogether proud of herself for being so "cool" around one of those strange-looking Muslim women.

Muslim Gal: also known as Jasmeet, but most people find that too difficult to say or they call her "Jasmine" like the Disney cartoon. Tired but not broken by the scrutiny of Americans like Cassie. Wears a burka.

V.O.: flight attendant. Very professional. Likes flying to Hawaii best.

(Lights up on Cassie stowing luggage in overhead bin. She sits; the seat by her is empty.)

V.O.
Ladies and Gentlemen, we will be taking off shortly. Your captain has requested that you fasten your seatbelts.

(Muslim gal enters)

MUSLIM GAL
Excuse me . . .

CASSIE
(looks up) Wha-oh! *(mouth open)* Oh! Hi.

MUSLIM GAL
Hi, yes, I am sitting here *(indicates her seat).*

CASSIE
Oh, yes, of course. I'm sorry, I'll just—I'll just get up.

(Cassie makes room for MUSLIM GAL awkwardly. MUSLIM GAL sits. Cassie sits and alternates between staring at her and looking away, all the while trying to hold it together.)

CASSIE
Can you believe how long it takes to get through the airport? Well, I suppose you would.

(beat) Do you want some gum? I have some because my ears pop *(digging in purse)* . . . oh, I only have one piece—do you want it?

MUSLIM GAL
No, please, you take it.

CASSIE
(oh, of course) Oh, I suppose you don't chew gum.

MUSLIM GAL
What?

CASSIE
What? *(beat)* My neighbor is Jewish. She's from—well, she says she's from Brooklyn Park, but I've been meaning to ask her where she's *from from,* you know?

MUSLIM GAL
I'm not Jewish.

CASSIE
Oh, yes, well and she doesn't have the *(gestures to burka).* That's very beautiful. Do you have hair? Underneath it?

MUSLIM GAL
(looks at her with disbelief) Yes. *(Cassie reaches for it)* Don't touch. Thank you. Please.

(They both sit uncomfortably for a while; MUSLIM GAL ignores CASSIE.)

CASSIE
So, do you have family in Afghanistan? Kabul, Afghanistan? It's really a shame how they treat the gals up-over-down-out there.

MUSLIM GAL
My family's from Indonesia.

CASSIE
Oh . . .

MUSLIM GAL
Jakarta.

CASSIE
What?

MUSLIM GAL
What?

CASSIE
What?

MUSLIM GAL
I'm a United States citizen. I was born here.

CASSIE
Oh, that's . . . *(beat)* You know we're not even going to get a meal on this flight? Nope, just a little bag of pretzels. *(leans in)* Cutbacks. That's why I always bring a sandwich *(starts shuffling through bag)*. Ohhhh . . . it's ham. It's a ham sandwich! I am so sorry!

MUSLIM GAL
That's okay. I'm not hungry.

CASSIE
Oh! I know this! I know this! It's the fasting holiday—the Ramada-da-Inn.

MUSLIM GAL
(amused) Ramadan.

CASSIE
Romulan.

MUSLIM GAL
Yes.

CASSIE
Yes! So you don't eat at all . . .

MUSLIM GAL
Just at night.

CASSIE
Like . . . a vampire.

MUSLIM GAL
What?

CASSIE
What?

MUSLIM GAL
It's actually not Ramadan right now. I'm just not hungry.

CASSIE
It's probably because you've messed up your metabolism. *(beat)* That explains a lot actually.

MUSLIM GAL
What?

CASSIE
If I was hungry all the time, I'd blow things up too.

MUSLIM GAL
Who are you?

CASSIE
I just want to punch something when my blood sugar drops.

MUSLIM GAL
(looks around nervously) I don't blow things up. No one I know blows things up.

CASSIE
(leans in) Yeah, and my family doesn't drink.

MUSLIM GAL
Okay.

CASSIE
Besides, what do I have to be proud of? Can you say Crusades?

MUSLIM GAL
Crusades.

CASSIE
That was very good. *(beat)* What do you think of Louis Farrakhan?

MUSLIM GAL
I think you're really confused.

CASSIE
Oh . . . well, you're probably not used to a woman who reads!

MUSLIM GAL
(almost sad) Why?

CASSIE
I suppose not. And here I am flashing my neck all over the place. *(wraps scarf over her head)*. There.

MUSLIM GAL
Please no—

CASSIE
I saw *Aladdin*.

MUSLIM GAL
No . . .

CASSIE
It was beautiful, even if it was a cartoon. *(singing)* Arabian nights . . .

MUSLIM GAL
(can't take it any more; calmly without touching her) Shhh! You have to stop that. *(pulls off scarf, folds it, hands it to her)* It's—it's against my religion for you to sing on a plane!

CASSIE
Oh!

MUSLIM GAL
You must remain absolutely silent. *(positions her facing away)* And face that way . . .

CASSIE

Towards Mecca?

MUSLIM GAL

(to keep her from speaking) Ah yes, yes. Mecca is that way and you must face it for the entire flight. We must remain absolutely silent or—or—Frodo will not save Middle Earth.

CASSIE

(turns back to her) I've heard of that.

MUSLIM GAL

Yes, yes you have. *(putting fingers to lips as if to a child)* Shhh . . .

CASSIE

Shhhh . . .

(beat)

CASSIE

(singing) I can show you the world! Shining, Shimmering, Splendid! Tell me, Princess—

MUSLIM GAL

That's it—I'm jumping!

CASSIE

(calls to her) Mazel Tov!

MUSLIM GAL

I'm not Jewish!

Copyright Brave New Workshop, 2004

Appendix 4
The Brave New Workshop, Yesterday & Today

Since 1958, our theatre has played a unique role within the community in which it exists. Our progressive and oftentimes irreverent shows have found a niche in a community that prides itself on reliable conservatism. We are a theatre that exposes and comments on things that most Minnesotans think about but rarely talk about. Most of what we do today is simply an extension of our founder's insight and intelligent sense of mischief. To help you clearly understand who the Brave New Workshop is, here is a brief history of how the BNW came to be.

Historical Timeline

1932	Dudley Riggs is born in Little Rock, Arkansas. He joins his family's circus as a performer at age five.
1950s	The advent of television causes the attendance of live performances to wane. Dudley and some of his fellow circus performers bring a new act to New York City, incorporating "audience input" into parts of the show for the first time. Calling themselves the Instant Theatre Company, the group brings the show to Chicago, Washington DC, and Burbank, California, before settling in Minneapolis.

1958	Dudley brings his Instant Theatre Company to Cafe Espresso on University Avenue in Northeast Minneapolis. His cafe/theatre houses the first espresso machine west of the Mississippi.
1961	The current style of comedy satire/satire revue shows is established, and the name Brave New Workshop is added.
1962	The first improv classes are taught to high-school students at the BNW.
1965	After mounting productions at Cafe Espresso on University Avenue, then moving to 207 East Hennepin Avenue, on November 30, 1965, Dudley and crew follow the muse to 2605 Hennepin Avenue, transforming a former bike shop into their permanent home. The ticket price of a BNW show in 1965 is $2. Also in 1965, current BNW owners John Sweeney and Jenni Lilledahl are born.
1970	The BNW International Touring Company is formed to take the BNW style of improvisation to college campuses and outlying Minnesota communities, as well as to other states and countries.
1971	Dudley opens a second theatre, the Experimental Theater Company (ETC) at 1430 Washington Avenue, in the Seven Corners area of Minneapolis. This theatre and cafe become home to other BNW productions, as well as stand-up comedy and variety acts. The 2605 Hennepin location continues to be the theatre's main stage. Dudley operates the ETC until 1991, when he consolidates his operations back to the single 2605 Hennepin location.

Mid-1970s	The BNW International Touring Company expands to include performances at conventions and for private businesses. This is the first time the BNW crosses over from stage to boardroom.
1975	The fourth annual New Year's Eve party at the BNW features a three-and-a-half-hour satirical comedy focusing on the low points of the year, as well as a buffet, all for the grand price of $8.50.
1990	The BNW celebrates twenty-five years at 2605 Hennepin by reducing ticket prices to the 1965 price of $2.
1997	John Sweeney and Jenni Lilledahl purchase the theatre from its founder, Dudley Riggs. The name of the historic theatre changes slightly to "The Brave New Workshop, founded by Dudley Riggs in 1958."
1997	The BNW signs a seven-figure contract to be the official comedy provider for the new Disney Cruise Line ships, the Magic and the Wonder.
1997	The BNW decides to aggressively expand its corporate services division, developing new corporate entertainment and training products and increasing its scope from less than fifteen events per year to more than one hundred.
1998	The BNW celebrates its forty-year anniversary by opening a new space for the theatre's main stage and offices at 3001 Hennepin Avenue in Calhoun Square.
1999	The Brave New Institute grows from seven students to a school hosting more than 250 students each week. It now has eleven teachers and fifteen class sections per week.

2000	The Brave New Workshop produces "Flanagan's Wake," an interactive Irish comedy at the 2605 Hennepin location. This production is in cooperation with the Noble Fool Theatre of Chicago.
2001	The BNW reaches another milestone when, for the first time in its history, it opens a theatre in a location other than Minneapolis. The BNW renovates the historic Palace Theatre at 17 West Seventh Place in St. Paul. In January 2001, the BNW opens this space with the Irish comedy "Flanagan's Wake."
2002	The BNW moves its mainstage operations back to the 2605 Hennepin Avenue theatre, once again establishing this location as its historic home.
2003	"Flanagan's Wake" closes after a successful two-year run, making way for "MN: It's Not Just for Lutherans Anymore!" which opens September 5 at the Palace Theatre space.
2005	Despite a poor economy, the Brave New Workshop continues to operate its theatre in the Twin Cities, an improvisational school of nearly 300 students, and a corporate services division with a reputation as a national leader in corporate entertainment, training, and keynote speeches.

As of this printing, hundreds of talented writer/actors have passed through our doors and have created approximately 252 shows of original sketch comedy for the BNW stage. Each and every sketch was developed using some version of the creative process outlined in this book. The eight secrets that were outlined in previous chapters have been present in our theatre since its beginning. Since President Truman, we have consistently produced some of the most stellar improvisation-based sketch comedy in the world.

After clearly defining our role as a cutting-edge creator of satirical comedy, our audiences began to ask if we could teach them the art of improvisation. As we began to share the history and philosophies of the BNW, the Brave New Institute was born. This led to the formal creation of our school. Over the years, that instructional part of our company has ebbed and flowed, going from casual improvisational "drop-ins" to our current eighteen-month curriculum. Along the way, we have accumulated, refined, and maximized the insights of the hundreds of actors and instructors who have expanded on Dudley's original improvisational model.

A third product line begged to be created in the early 1970s, as members of our audience began to request that our creative staff develop and perform business theatre sketches and songs for events outside the walls of our theatre. Those early shows were the beginning of what is now the most profitable division within our organization, our corporate services division. This wonderful byproduct of our original mission allows us to continue as a self-sustaining organization. Unlike most other arts organizations, we do not rely on federal grants or contributions. Currently, the corporate services division creates, produces, and performs more than one hundred corporate entertainment events per year.

In addition to providing clients with corporate entertainment, we have developed a world-class corporate training program. Since 1998, the BNW has consistently provided corporate improvisational training as a way to increase the innovation, teambuilding, acceptance of change, and leadership capabilities of the corporate world. Participants describe our corporate training as "innovative," "groundbreaking," "shocking," and an "outward bound for the mind." We attribute our success to the very nature of improvisation and our ability to help people learn commonly understood principles through an uncommon experience.

Undeniably, our history and philosophies have brought us to where we are today, employing all of the secrets of improvisation to run our business. We are not unrealistic about the challenges of making a small-budget, self-sustaining theatre successful. By practicing the secrets of improvisation, we have been able to create an uncommonly positive and innovative workplace.

*If you are interested in learning more about how the
Brave New Workshop can help you, your school,
or your theatre company to be more innovative, please go to:*

www.BraveNewWorkshop.com
or
www.artofthelaugh.com

Index

acceptance, 6, 12, 15, 46, 71, 143
accept all ideas, 12–18, 21, 22, 30, 51, 94, 95
accept all styles, 25–30, 71, 76
action (of the scene), 31, 60, 63, 64, 65, 72, 73, 101
actor, 3, 4, 6, 11, 14, 18, 19, 25, 37, 38, 44, 59, 62, 69, 70, 76, 77, 78, 89, 142, 143
Ad Game, 53
administrator, 4, 11, 81
aha moment, 4
artistic standards, 11
assignments, 83–86
audience, 3, 4, 6, 7, 11, 12, 13, 25, 31, 38, 49, 55, 59, 62, 63, 65, 66, 70, 73, 76–79, 81, 98, 99, 139, 143

Brave New Institute, 59, 90, 91, 141, 143

cast meeting, 82, 95
character, 6, 25, 29, 60–65, 67, 72, 73, 77, 88, 93, 94, 97, 98, 100, 101
Chavez, Cesar, 8
Clams Are Great, 45–46
clap, 36–37
Close, Del, 6, 7
collaboration, 31, 72, 73
Collins, Mo, 4
comedic tools, 66
commedia dell'arte, 7, 8
communication, 25–26, 32, 37, 38
Compass Players, 7
Conducted Story, 29
contradiction, 14
corporate services, 6, 141, 142, 143
costume, 63, 76, 78, 84, 85, 86, 101
costumer, 84
Count to Ten, 41
creative funnel process, 49, 69–81
creativity, 5, 6, 9, 11, 46, 49, 59, 78, 88, 89

"Das Bootylicious," 132
Declaration Lines, 32
declarations, 31–37, 49, 79, 96
defer judgment, 18–24, 70, 72, 88, 95
dialogue, 7, 25, 50, 60, 61, 64, 65, 75, 99
director, 4, 6, 11, 64, 65, 66, 74–79, 81, 82, 83, 85, 86, 87
"Disney Toilet," 129
draft, 64, 74, 75, 76, 79, 84, 85, 86, 103
"Dueling Bells," 128
"Dull Man Running," 103–21, 124

editor, 74, 83
eight secrets, 11–58, 69, 70, 81, 94, 142
El Teatro Campesino, 8
engineering, 75

environment, 13, 14, 17, 19, 33, 37–44, 49, 56, 63, 65, 66, 71, 72, 73, 75, 101
Everybody Go, 14
exposition, 65, 73
"Extreme Things," 129

fighting for, 63
focus, 25–30, 32, 36–37, 38, 41, 51, 71, 76–77, 82
focus group, 76–77
follow the follower, 38, 43
Franken, Al, 4
fuel, 6, 50, 54, 55, 77
fun-through, 85
funnel, 18, 49, 50, 69–81, 82, 88
funny, 12, 14, 18, 28, 30, 34, 49, 54, 61, 63, 65, 72, 87, 101
the "funny," 101

gift, 12, 20–22, 31, 34, 56
Group and Leaderless Mirror, 42
group mind, 42, 83

hell week, 78, 86
"Home for the Hostilities, Again," 128

idea generation process, 3, 4, 12, 18, 19, 38, 45, 50, 59, 60, 70
imperfection, 81
innovation, 4, 5, 6, 11, 44–49, 72, 81, 87–89, 143
insights, 11, 15, 16, 21, 23, 27, 30, 33, 35, 36, 37, 40, 41, 43, 46, 48, 51, 53, 55, 57, 89–98, 143
Instant Theatre Company, 7, 139, 140
interactive exercises, 11, 14, 16, 20, 22, 27, 29, 32, 35, 36, 39, 41, 42, 45, 47, 50, 53, 55, 56

"Jessie Goes to Hollywood," 123
Jiffy Pop, 49, 71
Johnstone, Keith, 6, 8
judgment, 18–24, 70, 72, 88, 95
jumping-off point, 35, 61–62, 70

key elements, 60, 61, 62–64, 65, 66, 71–75, 79, 84, 88, 99–101, 103

Letofsky, Irv, 4
Lilledahl, Jenni, xvi, 140, 141
Line Word Ball, 35
location, 61, 63, 101
lyrics, 84, 85, 88

MacNicol, Peter, 5
market, 19, 70, 77, 79, 80, 87
Master Inspiration List, 70, 71, 74, 75, 83
McEwen, Caleb, 128
McEwen, Katy, 129
McManus, Mike, 5
Minnesota Nice, 32
musical director, 83
"Muslim Gal," 132

Newsstand, 56–57

One-Word Story, 29, 55
opening night, 45, 69, 70, 75, 78, 79, 87
organic response, 39

pace, 16, 19, 22, 73, 75, 77, 85, 87, 101
Pass the Clap, 36

Pattern Game, 39
performance notes, 86, 87
Peterman, Melissa, 5
parodies, 67
playwright, 4, 6, 8, 81
point of view, 25, 30, 31–37, 49, 50, 60, 61, 62–63, 65, 83, 100
"Premium Arm," 123
pre-rehearsal, 82
Press Conference, 47–48
preview week, 77–78, 87
productivity, 4, 12, 25, 38, 66, 71
Proft, Pat, xv, 4
"Promiscuous Hostility, Positive Neutrality," 5

quality, 5, 13, 18, 19, 20, 32, 61, 66, 69, 70, 71, 74, 77, 78
quantity, 18, 70, 74

refinement, 71–72
rehearsal, 32, 61, 70, 75, 79, 81–87
reusable bits, 67
reusable characters, 67
reusable environments, 67
revue, 82, 140
reward system, 44–49
rewrite, 65, 66, 86
Riggs, Dudley, 4, 6, 7, 139, 141
risk taking, 44–49
road testing, 77–78
run-through, 86

satirical point, 60, 61, 62, 64, 65, 72, 73, 99–100
script writer, 59–67
secret 1, 12–18
secret 2, 18–24
secret 3, 25–30

secret 4, 31–37
secret 5, 37–44
secret 6, 44–49
secret 7, 49–54
secret 8, 54–58
setting, 60, 61, 63, 101
Shared (Two-Person) Story, 50
sharing focus, 25–30, 32, 71, 76
Shepherd, David, 6, 7
Sherohman, Tom, 4
show line-up, 86, 87
Shurtleff, Michael, 63
Sills, Paul, 6, 7
sketch comedy, 5, 18, 142
sketch worksheet, 64, 72, 73, 74, 99, 145
sketch writer, 4, 6, 59–67, 81
sketch-writing process, 61–67, 99
Sound and Motion Circle, 22
Spolin, Viola, 6, 7, 8
staff, 3, 4, 5, 18, 85, 143
statusless environment, 37–44, 75
Steen, Nancy, 5
style, 25–30, 32, 71, 76, 79, 83, 89, 101

tech week, 86
technical director, 83, 85, 86, 87
theme, 28, 61, 70–71, 82, 83, 84
"Tiger!", 103–21
timeline, 6–8, 139–42
Tolan, Peter, 4
tone, 45, 63, 77, 83, 101
tool, 6, 19, 66–67, 73, 74
trust, 6, 14, 19, 23, 27, 28, 30, 34, 37, 41, 54, 66, 79

Valdez, Luis, 8
vaudeville, 7

Walk in Space, 27
Wallem, Linda, 5
warm-ups, 83–86
Wexler, S., 103–21
Wexler, Shanan, 132
What Are You Doing?, 16
What's in the Box?, 20
writing process, 26, 59–67, 83, 91, 99, 145

Yarbrough, Cedric, 5
yes, and, 49
yes, first, 15, 49–54, 57, 58, 72, 73
"You Suck," 124
Young Actor's Company, 7

Content on Attached CD-ROM

To Assist You in Your Sketch Writing, Three Microsoft Word Documents:
1. Sketch Worksheet form.doc
2. Sketch Worksheet condensed.doc
3. The Condensed Writing Process.doc

For Your Reading Pleasure, Five Sample Scripts:
1. "Aptitude Test"
2. "Salt and Manna"
3. "Puppets"
4. "Ouch!"
5. "Khan"

For Your Listening Pleasure, Six Sample Songs in MP3 Format:
1. "Come Back"
2. "Salt and Manna"
3. "Ballad"
4. "Why I Love America"
5. "Waiting Around to Die"
6. "George W."

For Your Viewing Pleasure, Five Windows Media File Videos of Sketches Being Performed Live:
1. "Delaware"
2. "Infomercial"
3. "Ouch!"
4. "Fire"
5. "Janitor"

A teacher's guide for The Art of the Laugh *can be accessed by going to www.artofthelaugh.com*